Nellie's Journey

Mary Druce

Tellwell Talent
www.tellwell.ca

ISBN
978-1-77370-290-2 (Hardcover)
978-1-77370-289-6 (Paperback)
978-1-77370-291-9 (eBook)

Dedication:

For my father, George William Sutherland.
Who, at sixteen years of age, became a
boy soldier in the First World War.

In Remembrance of Andrea Main

Acknowledgements:

For all of my friends, family, fellow writing students
and instructors. Their helpfulness and comments
have been invaluable and very much appreciated.

CHAPTER ONE
The Family

Early Summer, 1914

The Parkin Family–Jessie, ("Mam"), Bill ("Pa"), George, Nellie, Sally and Will–had lived in the little house on Nanton Street for as long as Nellie could remember.

Sally was the pretty one, but Nellie was the good one. Mam had said so. "Nellie girl," she'd said, hands floury from working the dough, "You'll never hold a candle to that sister of yours for looks, but you are a good, wholesome girl, and clever, too, at that!"

Nellie knew that she was clever: clever and quick. Miss Pracket, her teacher, had told her four years ago that she was the brightest thirteen-year-old she'd ever had the pleasure of teaching. "If," she had said, "your parents can manage to keep you in school for another two years, why, we could easily get you into teacher's school; *easily*."

Pa had been so proud. "'Course we'll keep you in school, my girl. Won't we, Mam?"

Smiling, Mam had looked up from her ironing. Putting the flat iron carefully back on the heated stovetop, she had nodded her head in agreement. "'Course we will, Pa."

Sally, seated on a stool in the corner of the kitchen had been listening in as she did her darning. She had rolled her eyes. *What, she was thinking, is the use of cleverness?* The most useful thing to have–at least, for a girl–was beauty, and Sally had no doubt that she was on the way to being a great beauty. Everyone was saying so.

Still, she smiled fondly at her sister. There had to be *some* compensation for being plain and, she had to admit, that Nellie's cleverness had often covered up some of the childhood scrapes they had got themselves into–such as the time that a large ball of yarn, thrown in fun, had knocked Mam's beautiful teapot off the shelf. Mam had treasured that pot. It had been a present from her own Mam, now dead, and she had wept.

Although it was Sally who had done the throwing, Nellie had taken the blame for her younger sister and, eventually, following a scolding from Pa, things had been smoothed over.

The two girls had shared a tiny bedroom since first they had been old enough to leave the cradle in their parents' room. Nellie first, as she was the oldest by nearly two years. Together, lying abed, they had gossiped and giggled at the perceived oddities of parents, neighbours and fellow children, first those living on their street, and then later, once they had started school, their fellow students.

Mam had laughingly shaken her head at them. "What a pair of young mischief-makers ye are to be sure!" she'd said.

Now, at age seventeen and fifteen, they were still a team, gossiping merrily into the night until either Mam or Pa came up to scold them. "Sleep now, there's school tomorrow," they would say.

In the early morning, while the girls were still abed, they would listen to the sound of the front door closing as Pa and George left for work at the mill. Soon, their footsteps would be lost in the sound of wooden clogs clattering on the cobblestones as they joined the other workers, many of them women, hugging their shawls around them against the chill of morning.

Before the two girls left for school, Mam always insisted that they ate a good breakfast. "Growing girls need all the nourishment they can get. Boys, too," she'd added, with a glance at William, who was busy spooning down his porridge as though he had not been fed for weeks. None of the youngsters needed any encouragement to eat. They knew only too well how poor many of their neighbours were, and how hungry.

By the time that Nellie, now in her final year, and Sally left the house for school, the narrow streets were empty of the mass of workers who had preceded them earlier in the day. Sally, no scholar she, and a most reluctant student, dragged herself to school, while Nellie could hardly wait to start the day. The pair argued as they walked; Nellie urging her sister on, Sally dreaming of her Robert, lagging behind.

The pair navigated the long streets of huddled houses that were the living quarters of those who worked in the woolen mills of Eldenfield. Nellie teased Sally about her impossible dream–that of marrying Robert, the son of Sir Richard, owner of the mill–Sally, the while, insisting that Robert had been smitten with her ever since they first had met.

Busy with her daydreams, Sally noticed little of her surroundings, but Nellie, ever observant, could remember every detail, especially of how these dwellings differed from the grand places on the other side of town, the houses of the wealthier citizens, like that of Robert Hoyle and his family.

Mam was always telling the girls how lucky they were not to have to work long hours at the mill, at least, not yet. Many a time she had told them, "Your father worked real hard to get his promotion to foreman. With any luck," she would add, "you might never have to go to the mill at all.

"Imagine that! With a good education behind you, why, you could become almost anything: a shop girl at one of them big stores in the town, or maybe–" and here she would look fondly at Nellie "–even a teacher, as your Miss Pracket has said."

Sally had already decided what she was going to be: Mrs. Robert Hoyle. But Mam knew nothing about that, or about her secret meetings with the boy she had come to think of as "her" Rob.

They had met at the county fair, a rare day out into the countryside. While the men argued over the price of wool and the women brought forth their delicious baked goods, the youngsters, attracted by the sound of the fiddle, the clashing sticks and jingling bells of the Morris Men, had drifted towards the country dancing.

Nearly all the young men present had been ogling Sally with longing looks. But Robert, accustomed to having his own way, had got there first, and the pair had danced the afternoon away.

On the way home, Nellie had said quietly to her sister, "Sally, be careful, the Hoyles are a powerful family. You are so very pretty, I know, but we are just not in their league. Sir Richard will never allow his son to marry the daughter of one of his foremen, and Pa's job could be in danger."

Sally, always hating to be crossed and have her cherished dreams challenged, had immediately turned on her sister. Spitefully, she had told her in no uncertain terms that, as the plain old maid of the family, Nellie had no idea of what she was talking about. "Robert told me he thought I was the prettiest girl he'd ever seen, *and* that if ever he decided to become a married man, the girl that he married would look exactly like me. So put that in your silly old pipe and smoke it".

She had then hastened ahead, nose in the air, and had not spoken to her sister again for nearly a week.

Nellie, though hurt, had wisely said no more. She knew her sister, and knew too, that in due course, she would come and hug her, remorsefully apologising.

Nevertheless, recognising that her sister had been well and truly smitten, she had kept an anxious eye on the younger girl's comings and goings.

And, the meaning of the telling phrase "I would marry a girl who looked just like you," was not lost upon her. Sally, of course, flattered to the nth degree, would not have noticed the carefully hidden discrepancy buried within the young gentleman's declaration.

Fortunately, Robert had left for university shortly afterwards and so was no longer a present danger. In the meantime, however, Sally had substituted daydreaming for reality, building what Mam would have called "castles in the sky," and she was clearly beginning to firmly believe in her own wishful thinking.

*   *   *

The news was all over the place. The newspaper boys yelled it out at the tops of their young lungs. Those lucky enough to be in possession of a personal radio device huddled around the sets with their families. They were listening, through the crackling static, to the sober-voiced announcers, as they tolled out the news.

But mostly, it was done in the old, time-honoured way, from person to person, from door to door. "This nation is at war!"

"Dear God in Heaven!" Furiously, Mam slapped the damp teacloth on the kitchen table, making the two young men seated there shrink back from her wrath. It wasn't often that Jessie Parkin lost her temper so completely, but now she was fairly quivering with rage. A rage fuelled by fear.

"So, ye've signed up, the pair of ye, without so much as telling Pa and me about it. Wait 'til your Pa gets back from work, he'll have a few words to say to ye–especially you, George. What were you thinking of, encouraging our Willie to join up with ye? He is but fourteen years old. It's bad enough that *you're* going, but at least you're old enough to know your own mind."

"But Mam," William had tried to interrupt.

"Don't you 'Mam' me, young Willie. You're but fourteen years old and I'm going to march you right back there to those silly men what took you in the first place, just because you're a big lad. Couldn't they see that you are underage?"

"Mam." George stood up from the table.

"Don't you 'Mam' me neither, George! How could you, oh how *could* you ..." And quite suddenly, Mam collapsed, sobbing, at the table.

Gently, remorsefully, George wrapped his arms around her. "Hush now, our mam, I didn't know that Willie had enlisted. As a matter of fact, he got there before me, the silly young tyke". The proud smile that George now shot at his young brother belied his words.

"Yes, Mam." William, anxious to soothe his mother, broke in. "I knew that I ought to be nineteen, but everyone is saying that we have to go and fight for our country, and I *am* tall for my age. They say it'll all be over before Christmas and–and, well ... Oh, Mam, it will be such an *adventure*."

Now Jessie began to really wail. George shot his brother an exasperated look. William, abashed, sank back down in his chair.

By now, the two girls were home. Having caught the gist of what was going on, they stood together beside the kitchen table, ready to take their turn as comforters once George was done.

"Mam." Gently, George rubbed the heaving back of his mother. "I've got to go, I'm twenty years old and it's my duty as an Englishman. We might be invaded else. Everyone is saying so."

Slowly, Mam raised a tear-streaked face. Rubbing away the tears with the tea cloth still in her hand. She made a brave attempt at smiling up at her elder son. "Aye, lad," she said quietly, "ye've got to go, no doubt about it." But then, turning towards the younger boy, her gaze hardened. "*You* son, are *not* going to be going anywhere just yet. Yer Pa will see to that, I'll bargain".

"And exactly what," Bill Parkin's voice sounded from the doorway, "will I be seeing to, might I ask?"

Immediately, a scrabble of different voices broke forth to enlighten him.

Once everyone had settled down, and all were seated round the table, explanations were finally made. "I see," Pa said, sighing heavily. Then, putting his arm around his wife, he anchored her firmly to him, in case, perhaps, she might have been tempted to explode once more in angry tears.

Nodding at George, he said him, "Aye, son, ye must go. 'Tis your duty." George nodded back, and Nellie saw that her brother had become a man now, and was no longer just a young boy. Pa had accepted this and was treating him accordingly. She fought back her own tears, as the realization came to her that things were rapidly changing and that they would go on changing for some time. Her safe, known world was beginning to dissolve around her.

"As for you, young fellow," Pa turned to look at William, and Nellie wondered what might be coming next. With an *almost* twinkle in his eye, Pa declared, "You and I are going down to the recruitment office first thing tomorrow morn. We'll get you out of the mess you've managed to create for your young self. Agreed?"

Looking at his Mam, William swallowed hard, then quietly agreed. "Aye, Pa." he said. "Aye."

"Well, thank the Lord for small mercies." Mam gathered herself together. "We'll be having our supper as soon as I can get it going. Everyone, get your face and hands washed, right now."

Almost the same Mam as usual, Nellie thought, but not quite. She wondered how many other households around her were going through the same thing. A giant transition was taking place in people's minds, not just in Eldenfield, but throughout the country.

That night, as they settled into bed, Nellie tried to explain her feelings regarding this impending war to Sally. All that her sister seemed to be interested in, however, was whether or not her Robert would be signing up along with the other men. "I couldn't bear to lose him," she declared.

Nellie forbore to state the fact that, since his departure for university, her sister had hardly seen Robert at all. They just did not move in the same circles. Especially not since Sally, unequipped for anything better had, at the recommendation of her father, started work at the mill two months before.

As well, she noted yet again the fact that Sally seemed to be living in a dream world, to which she clung with a kind of desperate stubbornness. Further, Sally had not made any mention of her brothers having signed themselves up for war. Everything to her was "Robert, Robert, Robert."

Nellie had begun to worry about whether she would still be able to attend teaching school. With George, and eventually perhaps William, away at war, the Parkin family's finances might be considerably diminished. And, with most of the men gone from the community, the call would inevitably come for more women to take their places at the mill.

These thoughts gave her no pleasure at all, and between worrying about Sally's fragile hold on reality, and the worry about her own now uncertain future, she fell at last into an uneasy sleep.

CHAPTER TWO
A Problem with Sally

The morning sun shone brightly, dispersing the earlier mist.

The whole street had been transformed. There was bunting everywhere, draped from every window, door and street lamp. Gaily coloured Union Jacks adorned most front-parlour windows. The mill was closed for the day in order that the brave young recruits might be given a proper send-off.

Alas, it would be a send-off from which so many would not return ...

Everyone was dressed in their Sunday best, and though most of the women and even some of the men were near to tears, they were making a brave show in support of the young troops.

The band approached, gaily playing patriotic songs. Some of the older men, remembering other wars–Crimea, Afghanistan, South Africa–smiled in remembrance.

Others, also in remembrance–not of glory, but of lost comrades–did not smile.

And then the band rounded the corner and the cheers began. The young recruits marched proudly by, heads held high, backs stiff and straight, eyes to the front. So many young creatures in the flower of their youth, all so proud at having taken "The King's Shilling" of having signed up for the great adventure that they perceived war to be.

Mam and Pa–still holding on to young Willie, following their embarrassing trip to the recruitment office–and Nellie, were all anxiously scanning the horde of marching men, looking for a sighting of George.

Sally too was standing on tiptoe, craning her neck and with eyes darting hither and yon among the men. Nellie didn't need to make three guesses as to whom *she* was looking for.

Suddenly, there was a cry from Mam. "George! George!" And to the others, "There he is! There's our George!" The family began to clap and cheer, smiling and tearful at one and the same time.

George, of course, like the other men, was under orders to not respond, but he managed to make a slight inclination of his head, with a quick wink towards them as he passed. Then he was gone, hidden from view by the mass of men behind him.

Mam, like most of the other mothers around them, was in tears. The family gathered round to give her comfort. All, that is, except Sally.

Worried, Nellie had observed that her sister had been oblivious to the fact that George had been passing in front of them. And she didn't seem to be noticing now that Mam was in need of her comforting presence. Rather, she was swaying slightly and quietly murmuring to herself, "Oh Robert, my dearest, I will wait for you. I will wait."

From across the street, a flash of bright royal blue caught Nellie's eye. It was a very fine, very expensive hat set at a stylish angle upon the head of a *very* stylish and most expensive-looking young woman.

She stood out amongst the crowds of other women on the pavement who, though dressed in Sunday best, couldn't in Mam's words, "hold a candle" to her. Nellie realised, too, with a thrill of shock, that the girl looked almost the spitting image of their Sally. She, too, was scanning the endless parade of men, avidly looking for someone.

A cry rang out, as a fresh procession of marching men turned the corner into Nanton Street. "Robert! My Robert!" Now Sally was jumping wildly up and down. Her hat had flown off and, unheeding, she had trampled it underfoot. Her hair had fallen about her shoulders as, wild-eyed, she pushed furiously at the backs of the crowds in front of her, determined to intercept the man she had come to think of as her lover.

Robert Hoyle, oblivious in the midst of all the ambient noise going on around him, was searching, too. Now, his eye caught that of the elegant creature in the hat, smiling and waving at him.

Sally had become aware of the presence of this creature. As the pair across the street drew level, Robert, strictly against protocol, blew the young woman a kiss. She blew one back and, pushing against the crowd surrounding her, began to keep progress with the marching men.

The local people, unaccustomed to the presence of such finery among them, drew back respectfully, allowing her to pass.

And now, Sally began to make a great, roaring noise in her throat. The sound was more that of a wild beast than that of a young woman, and it stopped people in their tracks–all eyes on the extraordinary vision before them.

Sally roared again, a primitive, savage sound, as she began to push, furiously, against the crowd.

Mam gasped, "Sally!" her hands flying to her mouth as she watched in horror at the terrifying transformation taking place in her beautiful daughter.

No longer beautiful indeed, but like some she-demon. Face twisted into an ugly mask of fury, hair falling over her face and eyes, shoes fallen from her feet, she had twisted from Pa's grasping hand and continued on in pursuit of Robert and his creature.

Again, the crowd parted, but this time not in respect for an elegant lady, but rather, aghast at the frantic spectacle in their midst.

Somehow, she made it to the other side of the street, upsetting the marching rhythm of the men, until their sergeant major barked them back to order.

Drawing near to the Lady in Blue, she reached out to the startled woman, fiercely swatting the hat from off her elegantly coiffed head. Then, digging her nails into the fair skin of the woman's face, she raked them down from eye to chin.

As her perceived rival cried out in pain, a pair of strong arms were suddenly wrapped around Sally's waist, pinning her arms at her side.

Sally, thinking that this was a lover's embrace, burrowed her head into the uniformed breast, murmuring, "Robert, oh my sweet Robert."

Instead of the murmuring endearments she expected, Robert spat out "You *stupid* little witch. Where the hell did you get that idea from? How *dare* you attack my fiancé!"

"She got it from you, *sir*. She got it from you!"

Still holding tightly to Sally, now drooping in shock, Robert turned imperiously towards this interruption. Nellie was standing before him, quivering with rage.

"*You* encouraged my poor sister to think that you might be interested in her. *You*, and no one else." Then, acidly, she added, "I see that you have found your perfect lookalike, *sir*."

By now, two policemen had appeared on the scene, as well as a purple-faced sergeant major. "Back in line, sir, this instant," he barked commandingly. Reluctantly, Robert surrendered the limp body of Sally to one of the police officers.

Stopping only long enough to direct a withering look at the indignant Nellie, he blew a kiss towards his Lady in Blue, now safely on the arm of the second officer, before stepping back into the parade.

Sitting in the kitchen that night, Mam and Nellie were drinking from a pot of tea–the great British comforter. Words were by now exhausted, and Nellie was suddenly aware of the sound of the old clock ticking away the minutes. She had never thought of it before; there was usually so much bustle and conversation going on in this most comfortable of rooms. Now, for the moment, there were only the two of them.

Tears and self-recriminations–"How could we not have seen what was happening with her?"–were over with. George, of course, was gone and Pa and Willie were still at the hospital, answering questions from both doctors and police.

Breaking into the silence, Mam said quietly, "Well, girl, I suppose things are going to be very different now." And Nellie had had to agree that most definitely, they would.

With a sinking heart, she bid a silent farewell to her hopes and dreams of scholarship, and set her mind to accepting the fact that there would be no escape now. She would have to join the other workers labouring down at the mill.

*   *   *

Nellie stopped in mid-stride. Breathing heavily from the climb up from the tram terminus, now far below, she paused for a moment to take in the scene before her.

"Beautiful," she breathed.

Here, outside the town had been a place of respite, of escape from the grind of daily living, for not only herself, but her entire family, for as long as she could remember. She smiled again as she recalled sitting on her father's shoulders as he strode up towards the summit.

George, still just a boy back then, but determined to show himself as manly, had been keeping pace with Pa, while Mam, holding on to the two younger children, had laughed in delight. All of them revelling in the crisp air, the sun reaching its fingers down upon them in blessing, the musical chattering of the birds upon the branches.

It had always, and even now, seemed like living in a shining piece of heaven, while far below, the town ground on about its business.

Now, Nellie–alone, but happy for the moment to be so–shook free of her scarf and hat. Her long wavy hair ("Your best asset my girl, I'll tell you that for now't" Mam would say) tumbled over her shoulders.

The wind, catching it, blew the hair over her face and she laughed. "Beautiful," she said again, and, taking a deep breath of the clean, cool air of spring, she stretched luxuriously, before continuing with her ramble through the wooded hillside.

It had been a long, hard winter, but now in this early spring, the trees had begun to unfurl their buds and soon, she knew, that exquisitely delicate tracery of bustling greenery would be on display, a prelude to the denser green of summer. It seemed to her that hope–a hope long absent from 85 Nanton Street–must soon return.

After an hour or so of walking and breathing her fill, Nellie turned, making her way reluctantly down the hill, towards the tram terminal. She must hurry; already she could see the horses approaching, pulling their burden behind them.

The euphoria that had been abundantly evident all over Britain in the early days had long since disappeared, along with the flags, the bunting, the marching bands and the singing.

The oft-repeated words, "It will be over by Christmas," now had a hollow ring to them. This, especially so since the telegrams had begun to arrive.

Mothers, hearing the ring of the telegraph boy's bicycle, would stand motionless in mid-chore, thinking: *Oh God, let it not be my door that he comes knocking at. Please, dear God.* There would be a huge sigh of relief as the bell passed by, followed by feelings of intense guilt as, from farther down the street, the wailing would begin.

So far, there had been little news, except for the very occasional letter from George.

"No news is good news," Mam would say determinedly, but as she and Pa exchanged glances, there was a haunted look in both their eyes.

Sally was home again now, on leave from the asylum, after six months away. The doctors were very pleased with her progress they said. They had tried the new electric shock treatment and, from the wild creature that had arrived on their doorstep in September, she was now "Pleasingly docile."

Mam was *not* pleased. "T'aint our Sal," she would hiss at Pa. "'T'aint her at all. What have they done to her?" and her lips would quiver as she fought back the ever-ready tears.

At night, with her sister lying close by her, Nellie would try to revive the pleasant chats from their time before. It was of no use; Sally just wasn't the old Sally at all. She would smile benignly, and then continue gazing into space, unfocussed, unresponsive.

"Neurasthenia," the staff at the hospital had said and, then, smiling, attempting to be of comfort, "typical of a disappointed woman, you know." Mam and Pa listened attentively, impressed by the jargon, but none the wiser.

Nellie, however, had her own ideas. She sensed the benign contempt hidden beneath the words of these medical men; a contempt springing, however well-meaning, of the female sex. *Poor dears*, they seemed to be saying, probably thinking of Byron's "Love, to a man is a thing apart/'tis woman's whole existence."

Nellie could feel something like a fury developing within her. She, and all of her gender were being dismissed. However kindly meant, as in the case of the doctors, or contemptuously dismissive by the likes of Robert Hoyle, they were wrong, wrong, *wrong*.

Somehow, someway, she was going to prove them wrong. For the moment, she wasn't at all sure how she was going to manage it. But she *would* find a way. After this war, it was going to be a new world. She'd had an inkling of these feelings standing on the hillside the other day. Now she knew that she must find a way to join in the struggle for a better existence.

Reaching across, expecting nothing, she groped for Sally's hand. "Sal, I'm going to find a way to help you out of this. I *promise*."

And now, amazingly, Sally responded by tightening her grip on Nellie's hand. A faint whisper came back to her. "Yes, my Nellie. Thank you."

And now Nellie knew that her journey had begun. Her heart lifted and sang.

CHAPTER THREE

At the Western Front

George was sitting, pen in hand as he gazed over the bleak prospect before him. There was, for the moment, a brief break in the fighting, and George, with his fellow soldiers, was grateful.

Chewing anxiously on the end of his pen, he stopped, half smiling, remembering Mam's voice. "That don't do you no good, young George," and, "People will think I ain't feeding you proper."

He sighed. It was Mam, and, of course, Pa, to whom he was attempting to write. But what could he say? Certainly not anything about the kind of life he was living now. If, indeed, you could call it a life at all.

Looking out from the trench where he and his comrades were uncomfortably huddled, all he could see for acres around was nothing but desolation–just mud, dead and wounded trees, abandoned tanks and guns. And still, several bodies–those of German, Brits and French–had been left like so much detritus, lying half-buried in the mud.

Thank God, he thought, the ambulance people had managed to collect the wounded during this break in hostilities. He had watched as the gallant bearers trudged through the sucking, oozing mud–mud that had once been green and pleasant pastures for the animals of the neighbouring farms. Alas, the animals had long since gone, and the farms themselves were reduced now to rubble.

Gently, the bearers had gathered the wounded–some silent in their pain, others wailing for their mothers. Prising them out from the sucking mud, they had carefully lifted these precious burdens and laid them on to the makeshift stretchers.

One could hear the gently reassuring voices: "There, lad, we'll soon have you away from here. The medics will have you fixed soon enough. There, there ..." There would be a collective sigh, as two bearers would exchange glances. Glances that said, more eloquently than words, *"This one's gone."* And, of necessity, they would have to tip him in favour of another wounded.

George understood well enough that this was necessary. The wounded were the priority. The dead would have to wait until later. He knew, too, that the rats would already be tucking into their feasting, eating the very flesh that had, until just moments ago, been living, breathing and thinking men.

No, he could not write about this to his parents. Especially not to Mam. She would be heartbroken.

Instead, he would write yet again, as he had become accustomed to do, a complete fantasy of how "Our brave and gallant warriors" were cheerfully beating the living daylights out of the dastardly enemy.

It made him sick to his stomach to have to resort to such fabrications, but then he thought of the faces seated around the kitchen table at home. They would be listening as Pa, glasses perched on the end of his nose, read aloud.

He could just see Mam's face shining with pride as she pictured her son, trim in his clean and smartly pressed uniform, marching across the green turf of France and pushing the "dastardly enemy" before him.

He could see, too, Nellie's grave, attentive face, knowing that she would most probably see through his ruse, but also that she would understand completely the reason for it.

Sally, he could picture, too–a picture drawn for him in the letters from Nellie. Poor Sal. Her restless fingers would be twitching on the tabletop, her eyes vacant and far away.

He could hear Pa's voice break every now and again, and knew that he would suspect the truth behind his son's words. Yes, Pa would not be easily deceived.

George's worry now was for young Will. He would be listening in rapt attention, longing for the time when he could sign for the King's Shilling, and join in triumph with his brother in France.

Sighing, torn between guilt at the false impression he would be giving his younger brother–*God, don't let him sign up early like so many of the young lads here*–and the desire to protect his family from the worst, George picked up his pen once more and proceeded to write.

CHAPTER FOUR
At the Mill

"Ooh ..." Nellie stretched out her aching back. Straightening, she met the eye of the woman who was currently supervising the new young workers at the mill.

"Time for a short break, m'girl." The briskness of the voice belied the twinkle in Mrs. Hodge's eyes.

Nellie liked her–a kindly enough soul to those who proved their worth, but stern enough to those who lagged, or daydreamed.

Nellie admired the way that Alice Hodge dispatched her work with a will. She had no choice, of course, with a husband killed in the aftermath of the South African war, and with three growing children to raise, she raced through her work with a dedicated fury of speed that sometimes made Nellie drop her jaw in admiration.

Once, when Nellie had questioned this energy, Alice had declared, "The more ye work, the better do ye be paid." And surely, she needed every penny to keep her family together: housed, clothed and fed. "There'll be no workhouse for us," she had declared aloud more than once.

Workhouse. This was a word spoken in dread. "End of the road warehouse" might best describe these cold and ugly places.

People with nothing between them but the shared experience of utter poverty, were here given a meagre bed, a poor diet and a roof over their heads, all in exchange for whatever work they could manage.

Few ever escaped this cycle of poverty into which they had fallen, and so died and were buried in a common grave. With no memorial to remember them by, they were soon forgotten. It was as though they had never been.

Remembering the eye-opening experience it had been for her, reading Dickens' *Oliver Twist,* Nellie shuddered. Looking over at Alice Hodge, already back at work, busily picking and threading, pushing back the occasional stray hair escaping from under her cap, Nellie's face softened. She was thinking about the many women left behind, looking after their dead men's children. Men dead from the Boer War, Afghanistan, the Crimea ... And now, this war, that everyone had said would be over and done with before Christmas.

No, it was no wonder that people–husbandless women with children in particular–feared the dreaded workhouse.

Thinking of Dickens, how well he knew, from his own experience, the predicaments of his characters, Nellie felt a pang at the loss of time she had these days for her reading and writing.

Of course, it had been inevitable that she would have to find work of some kind, now that George was away. Mam had enough to do at home, for Sal could not be left alone for long. Sally could do no work, and Will earned very little as a pot boy at the Lion's Head, the local inn.

Pa had been worried, too, given the insult to the Hoyle family in his daughter's assault on Robert's fiancée, that he might lose his job.

Thank goodness, though, that this calamity had not come to pass. Sir Richard had been only too aware of the unfortunate character traits possessed by his son and had taken the time to send someone down to the mill to inform Pa that his job would be safe.

In addition, he had added the offer of a job for Nellie, should she be seeking work at this time.

Bill Parkin was man enough of the world to understand that these offers were not solely due to Sir Richard's kindness of heart. With so many of the young men leaving to fight, there was a growing need for replacement workers.

Who better then, to fill the gaps than older men with a family to provide for, and young women fresh from school? Nevertheless, he accepted gratefully, albeit with a heavy heart at the loss of Nellie's dreams.

And so, Nellie, with a smile on her face to allay her father's fears for her, had started at the mill. Resolutely turning her face from the direction of school, she set herself to learning the intricate work involved in the weaving of cloth.

It had not taken her long to pick up enough skill to be able to manage, almost automatically, the process involved. Soon, this process had become familiar enough that she was able to detach her mind from time to time, in order to plan for her eventual escape.

She was not sure how this might be achieved, but knew with every fibre of her being that one day it would be so.

In the meantime, under Alice's tutelage, her fingers flew faster and faster, creating the warp and weft, the along and across of producing cloth.

Really, it was just like knitting: across and through, up and down. This was something with which she had been familiar since the age of four, learning to make socks, hats and scarves for herself and family.

Much harder to cope with, though, was the almost unbearable noise made by these huge new machines as they clattered furiously, responding to the pace of many women working.

Conversation was impossible, and had to be conducted "on the fly" during the few, too-short breaks allowed. Hard on the feet and back, too, she thought ruefully, bending to rub her aching back.

"Daydreaming, lovie?"

Alice, smiling, had touched Nellie's arm. Startled, Nellie scrambled to attention, apologising for her tardiness.

"Sorry, Alice," she mouthed. Then more forcefully, in order to be heard above the noise, "I was just ... thinking."

"S'alright, pet. I'm often thinking to myself, too. How things might have been different, shall I say."

Again, she had brushed gently at Nellie's shoulder, her way of communicating that she knew and understood the pain of broken dreams.

Nellie had smiled her thanks before turning away her head, hiding the tears that threatened to flow. Furiously, she bit her lip, determined not to follow the almost overwhelming instinct to throw herself into the motherly arms, surrendering herself to crying until she could cry no more.

The thought of her father, however, struggling to keep his family together and as cheerful as possible, gave her strength to resist any such dissolution on her part. She knew that he relied on her as his "second in command" on the home front. She must not let him down.

Pulling herself together, she set herself back to work with a will– not noticing, even, the look on the other woman's face as, nodding her approval, she, too, picked up the threads of her work.

For a while, the two women worked on, fingers flying. Conversation of any real moment was impossible, both above the clacking of the looms and the necessity of focussing intently upon the work at hand.

Nellie could feel, however, the waves of sympathetic understanding coming to her from Alice. She felt immensely cheered by the thought of having found a true friend–someone from outside the family, who might just have a different perspective to offer her.

CHAPTER FIVE

Alice and Family

"Would you come home wi' me, lass? Mebbe meet some of the family and have a nice hot cup o' tea and a wee bit of a chat?"

It was a Saturday evening, and they were shutting down for the day. Alice peered at Nellie's pale face, the dark shadows under her eyes. "Eee, lass, ye look as though y'could do wi' a wee bit of a change."

She was right, of course. Life at home was not getting to be any easier. Despite Nellie's efforts, Sally was sinking into a deeply apathetic state.

She would sit, motionless, for hours on end–the only sign of life her fingers endlessly twitching and chittering over the tabletop. If she responded to any attempts by the family to engage her in cheerful conversation, the response would be brief and distracted.

After which, she would return to her state of inertia, in which state she would remain until prompted to eat or to sleep.

Hearing the news from the Front–this coming from the gossip of returning, wounded soldiers and passed on by their horror-stricken families, the awful truth of war was beginning to filter through to the general public. Mam, like so many others, despite the falsely cheerful letters from George and the continuing grandiose newspaper accounts, was also becoming increasingly disillusioned. Her ideas of the grandeur of the war effort had become considerably modified.

As far as Sally was concerned, Will too, after a few months of brotherly teasing and prodding, had given up trying to break through his sister's inertia. Perplexed at her lack of response, his mind was turning more and more to the time when, in a month or two, he would be celebrating his fifteenth birthday.

Still much short of nineteen, he had been hearing rumours that the age requirements were being ignored. Enthusiastic youngsters were being allowed–even encouraged–to sign for the King's Shilling, and they were responding in droves.

Filled with the desire for adventure, and with the optimism of youth telling them that nothing too bad would happen to them, they were lining up at the recruitment offices and being kindly received.

Pa, Nellie had noticed, had recently begun to look even more tired and worn with worry. She understood that it was essential that she should remain strong and put up a cheerful front, in order to give him the support he needed.

All of this was taking its toll on her, however, and now, considering Alice's invitation, she was only too happy to accept.

The tiny kitchen was immaculate, dishes washed and stacked, towels neatly folded, floor swept and scrubbed.

Nellie looked around in admiring awe. "How do you manage all this *and* work so hard and long at the mill?"

"Oh, my young ones." Alice smiled. "They all three of them take their turn in helping out and, well, it's our Penny who organises them of course, she being eighteen now, y'know."

There was pride in her voice as she continued listing her children for Nellie's benefit. "Gareth, our Gary, is but sixteen, but he knows he is the man of the house now and helps out as much as he can. Does very well, too, despite he works all hours in the stables at t'Lion's Head." She sniffed. "And little enough he's paid for it an' all!

"Still," she continued, a shadow falling across her face, "rather here than over there."

She paused, and Nellie recognised the look on her face, the tremor in her voice–it was the same as her Mam's when speaking of Will. Instinctively, she reached across the table, just as she was wont to do for her mother, and grasped the other woman's hands in her own.

Nodding her thanks and recovering her equilibrium, Alice gently withdrew her hands, putting them in her lap before continuing. "He loves the horses does our Gary–says that when he takes the King's Shilling, he will apply to work with the horses instead of being a foot soldier."

Here, she paused again, gulping at the thought of her only son going off to war.

There was, for a moment, such a forlorn look upon the older woman's face that Nellie had to restrain herself from rushing around the table and giving her a hug.

She realised however, that as an older woman, Alice would need to retain her dignity in front of someone much younger than she.

Almost to herself, Alice murmured, "Dear God, I hope this dreadful war will be done and over with before he comes of age."

Lord, Nellie thought to herself, *it's the same everywhere. Every household in the land is suffering, just like Mam, just like Alice.*

At the same time, her heart swelled with pride that this stalwart woman had felt able to show the extent of her pain in this way. *We really are good friends now,* she thought.

Suddenly, she became aware that the kettle on the stove, placed there by Alice when they had come in, was now bubbling furiously, practically dancing where it stood.

Jumping to her feet and assuming a briskly cheerful voice she cried, "Right then, Alice. Let's have that cuppa tea!"

Then, as Alice, hands pushing down on the tabletop, began to rise, she said, "No, no, I'll see to it. You just sit there and rest yourself for a change."

Gratefully, Alice subsided, briskly wiping her eyes with the edge of her apron. Smiling now, she watched as Nellie busied herself with kettle, teapot and cups.

Soon, they were seated companionably opposite one another again, cups of steaming comfort before them.

"Where are your children now?" Nellie asked. "Tell me about them."

"Well..." Between sips, Alice began to count them off on her fingers. "There's Penny of course, she's working at Brombridges–that nice dress shop on the other side of town." She made a rueful face, saying, "Place where all the nobs shop. The likes of us'll never be able to shop there."

"Does she enjoy the work?"

"Oh yes, she loves beautiful things and has a good eye for style. She's good with people, too, and knows how to please. They really like her there I'm glad to say, and though the pay aren't too much, it's enough to help us out a bit."

She smiled to herself, obviously thinking of her clever, beautiful daughter. Nellie was touched once more by this likeness in Alice to her own mother.

"And the others?" she prompted.

Snapping out of her reverie, Alice went on. "Oh, ah, yes. Well now, I've told you about our Gary and how he loves the horses so." A cloud passed briefly across her face, but then she continued. "As I said, he's sixteen now, he'll turn seventeen later on this year, and so he won't turn nineteen until 1918. The war ought to be well over long before that."

Satisfied with her own decision as to when the war would be done with, Alice smiled. Settling back in her seat, she drained her cup and set it firmly back on the table. The Kaiser would just have to lump it. Alice had decided and that was that.

Nellie smiled fondly at her feisty friend. "And your third?"

"Aye, oh, aye. Our Izzie, our young Isobel. Well, she's but fourteen just now, but growing fast. A little sweetheart she is, though I say it meself, as shouldn't." She smiled to herself, as though to belie the implied self-criticism of her comments.

"Aye, well, sometimes of a Saturday, she'll stay over for supper wi' her Auntie Liz and her Granny Hodge. They're just the next street over–she'll be back soon. They just love her, though, them two. Well, they never got over the loss of our Bert, and the children are a joy to them."

"And Bert was Granny Hodge's son?"

"Aye, and Liz was his sister. Aye, my poor Bert–he never got to see his children grow. He would have been proud of them I know."

Alice paused for a moment, a wistful look on her face. Once again, Nellie felt the desire to hug her, as she would have her mother. She was glad, at least, to be a listening ear to this woman who had befriended her.

"He was abroad when he died?"

"Aye, lovie. He got took in South Africa. He'd been in the war against the Boers, and had hardly a scratch to show for that." Alice sighed before continuing. "No, it weren't the war that took him in the end."

She looked across the table at Nellie, who nodded encouragingly.

"He'd had a small wound to the knee, but were much better by the time he got back home to us, scarcely a limp in him. Excited he were–wanted us to move over there with him and settle down on some sort of a farm. He'd been offered a job there, y'see."

She faltered for a moment, biting her lip. Again, Nellie nodded for her to go on.

"I didn't want to go to foreign parts–not with the children, and wars and foreigners and all that. So, I said to wait a bit and we'd talk about it mebbe, and decide later."

This tale was obviously proving difficult to tell. Alice, sighing, rubbed her hands over her face before continuing.

"He got his old job back and worked for a couple of years. In the end, though, I could see how tired he was of grinding away at the mill–his heart just weren't in it. He longed for the wide-open spaces and the opportunities of that far-away land."

Again she sighed, pausing for a moment as she remembered her husband's dream.

"So I said yes, go and see what you can make of it there if the offer is still on. Well, it were–the offer I mean. They wanted as many of us Brits over there as would come. So, in 1904, he went."

The plan were for him to settle down in the job and then send for us. But scarce had he been there for a couple of months when the news came that he were dead. Kicked in the head he were–be a horse! All the way through that war, with scarce a mark on him, and then to die because of a bloomin' horse!"

Once again, Nellie found herself wanting to comfort this woman with some kind of physical touch. However, before she could make a move, Alice had once more summoned up her remarkable strength.

Blowing her nose, she straightened up in her chair and continued. "Granny Hodge and Auntie Liz were a boon to me then. Despite their own grief, they rallied round, taking on the care of the children while I went back to work at t'mill. Been there ever since."

Nellie, filled with admiration, declared, "Alice, dear Alice, you are a most remarkable woman!"

"Eee, Lass." Alice began to laugh, then said, "As I've said many a time to ye, you do what y'have to do and"–her voice hardened–"you have to keep out of the workhouse, for that is a place of iniquity. There's no doubting that."

Testily, she threw up her arms in disgust. "What, I would like to know, is why in God's name did we have to bother with them Boers in the first place? South Africa, indeed. Too, too far away and none of our business. That's my opinion and I'm sticking to it."

Wisely refraining from getting into the complicated subject of politics, Nellie asked, "When will they be back? The children, I mean?"

Coming down from her high horse, Alice smiled ruefully. "Eee, I'm sorry love. Sometimes the stupidity of men gets me going like. I think it's we women what should be doing the ruling. I really do."

Nellie wasn't sure that she agreed, but stayed quiet as Alice continued.

"As for our Penny, she should be on her way home on the tram by now. They've been stock-taking all this week–no extra pay, mind!" She snorted in disgust, shaking her head.

For a moment she paused, considering the ills that beset the working man and woman, all at the mercy of their employers. Then, smiling, she picked up on the litany of her children.

"Well, now, Gary stays with the horses, feeding and grooming, until the last travellers have arrived and settled in. His hours, depending on how busy things are, are topsy-turvy. We expect him when we see him and don't worry too much if he's late. Sometimes I go and fetch Izzie from our Gran's, but I told them that I might take a little while longer than usual. Liz'll bring her soon enough."

At that moment, the clock on the wall began to chime the hour. Eight of the clock. Nellie started to her feet.

"Oh, Alice, I'd love to stay and meet them all, but it'll have to be another time. My family will be worried by now–I'm never usually late."

Alice put out a restraining hand. "Aye, lass, o'course. But if y'wait just a moment more, there's something I've been intending to speak to you about."

Nellie, with an anxious glance at the clock, subsided obediently. Alice reached across to take the younger woman's hands into her own, work-worn ones.

"My Bert, before he went back abroad, had thought to begin going to the weekly lectures–a kind of working man's educational club at the library on the other side o'town. He'd thought to improve his understanding of things like. A good idea, really."

Nellie nodded, again glancing at the clock.

"Well, now," Alice continued, "our Penny's been thinking the same thing. Y'see, the library's not far from Brombridges, where she works, and I were thinking that if you were to go with her, then y'could both come home together on the late tram.

"You and she would enjoy one another's company, I know. The pair of ye are so alike–as bright as two shiny buttons. 'Tis a great pity to waste good minds. It's too late for an old bird like me, but I'd just love to see the pair of you getting on in the world."

Looking at Alice's face, so earnest, so full of hope, Nellie felt her own hope rising. Gently disengaging herself from the older woman's grasp, she rose to her feet.

Looking down at the woman who was now so much of a friend to her, she smiled.

"Why not, Alice dear," she said. "Why not!"

CHAPTER SIX
A Friendship Blooms

It was cold and raining as the two young women stepped out from the library and into the street. The pavement was slick with rain, and the puddling forced the pair to lift their skirts in order to keep them dry.

During the course of the last month or two, and with their shared interest in learning, Penny and Nell had become fast friends.

Nellie had found these sessions to be a splendid antidote to not only the drudgery of working at the mill, but also as a respite from the melancholic atmosphere pervading her home at this time.

Will had turned sixteen in August and, with the lax new rules, there were no longer any excuses for him to not sign for the King's Shilling. He and Pa had gone together down to the recruitment office, where, much to his satisfaction, he had been warmly received.

To his chagrin, Pa had furiously argued the toss with the recruitment officer at the desk. "He's only a lad–it'll break his mam's heart. What's wrong wi' this country of ours, taking youngsters that are scarce out of their childhood."

It was of no use. The officer had been adamant. The country needed fit young men, and Will filled the requirements nicely.

Mam's anger knew no bounds. She was terrified, and threatening to write to the king, telling him to stop this nonsense at once.

It took all of Pa and Will's powers of persuasion to stop her from carrying out this threat. The country was at war, things were not going well. An invasion from Germany must be headed off at the pass, and that was that.

The very next day, clad in his khakis and with his pack on his back, Will had set off, head held high and marching–at his own request–entirely alone, all goodbyes having already been said at the door of 85 Nanton Street.

No marching bands or cheering crowds for him. He had turned the corner and, with a final wave, had disappeared from view.

His parents had wept, giving full vent to their grief. Sally, vaguely disturbed by the unhappiness now pervading the room, had rocked from side to side, murmuring, "He's gone. Oh, my Robert, he's gone." A shadow of puzzlement had crossed her face, then "Not my Robert!" A sigh and then, raising her head and straightening her shoulders, "Not *my* Robert!"

Following Will's departure, Nellie found herself gravitating more and more to the Hodge household, where the very seams of the house seemed to radiate happiness.

Often, she had found herself feeling guilty at this desertion, but as Alice assured her, "Eee, lass, y'need to keep hold of your sanity. You'll help your family much better if ye can stay strong."

This was true, Nellie reflected, and when she was at home, she made a special attempt to inject some liveliness into the Parkin household.

Sally, she noticed, seemed to be becoming more responsive. Reaching out between their beds one night, as Nellie was making her usual comforting conversation, Sally had grasped her sister's hand murmuring, "Oh, my dear Nell." Then, as Nellie turned to her in wonderment, she had settled back into her bed, very quietly murmuring again, "Dear Nell, dear Nell," before falling into a sound sleep.

There had been no more actual murmurings, but with a renewed hope in her heart, Nellie had continued with these rather one-sided, nocturnal conversations–with Sally smiling, and very occasionally nodding and reaching for her hand.

Fearing to raise hopes that might be so easily dashed, Nellie had said nothing of this to either Mam or Pa. Tempted as she had been, she refrained also from telling anything of this to either Alice or Penny. But still, there had been a small, bright flame of hope in her heart, as she considered the fact that she just might be doing some good for Sally.

Now, with Penny beside her, sloshing through the rain towards the tram stop, the two girls were chatting animatedly. "My, Nell, that were interesting." Penny was bubbling with enthusiasm.

"Yes." Nellie smiled down at her friend. "There is certainly more going on in this world than we had ever thought about before." Then, her brow furrowed. "They are right y'know–these people that are protesting our conditions. I really hadn't wondered why people didn't protest. I suppose we've all been just too busy, with our noses to the grindstone. Look at my Pa, and look at our poor Mams."

"Aye." Penny's enthusiasm had begun to subside. Her pace slowed as she frowned in thought. Then, worriedly, she said, "I'm not sure how much longer she can go on at this pace. She rarely gets enough rest, and she worries about Gran getting older. And then there's the housework and the worry about what's going on at the Front."

"And then there's our Gareth. He's right set on going over there, y'know. He's tall for his age. Just like your Will, they'd take him like a shot. They are just glad to get the manpower. Well, and our Gareth just *loves* them horses. Just like they were his children."

Nellie nodded in sympathy. Then, returning to their discussion, she said, "Aye, and all this trouble in Ireland, wanting Home Rule, and people demanding–not asking, mind, but *demanding*–better working conditions. Some say we could soon be having a civil war."

"*Really*?" Penny sounded shocked.

"Yes." Nellie was thoughtful. "Yes, well, what our lecturer was talking about tonight, I suppose, bears that idea out. There seems to be so much seething protest going on just underneath the surface."

"Mmm." Penny was thoughtful. "And all these shifting alliances between nations. The way that–what did he call it? Yes, the triple alliances of Britain and the Empire with France and Russia, versus the central powers of Germany and Austria-Hungary ..."

"Um," Nellie, interrupting, took up the litany. "But the *history* of it all is so interesting. The way he described how these alliances began in, um ..."

"1815," Penny supplied.

"1815." Nellie nodded her thanks. "And this was all, initially, intended to keep the peace!"

"Yes." Penny sighed. "As Mr. Franks was saying, everyone was so sure that peace would be kept. And now look at us, with everyone declaring war on everyone else."

"And"–Nellie stopped for a moment in her tracks–"all of this fighting, this jockeying for power was–seemingly, at least–started by a madman shooting the Archduke Ferdinand and his wife at Sarajevo."

"Ooh." Penny, fascinated by this, nodded vigorously. "Do you ... do you think that that could all be part of a *plot?*"

Nellie, intrigued, asked, "What sort of a plot?"

"Well, it's certainly come at a good time, hasn't it? Now our minds are all taken up by the war. Our men are being killed and maimed–and what *for*? For some stupid war that us ordinary folks didn't want in the first place."

The two friends, now nearing the tram stop, had been so engrossed in their conversation that they had failed to hear the heavy-booted footsteps coming up behind them.

Now, suddenly, a pair of rough hands seized them by their collars. They gasped as a large policeman, red of face, spun them round to face him. Grimly, he glared into each of their faces in turn.

"Ach, you stupid young wenches! What do the likes of you know anything about anything? Why are y'out here at night anyway? Ye should be at home, attending to yer domestic duties. I've a mind to arrest the pair of y'ese as common prostitutes, if not downright disturbers of the peace."

Penny, in shock, began to whimper, but Nellie, feeling once again the now familiar rage that injustice seemed to elicit from her, drew herself up to her full height. Grasping the man's hand, she tore it from her neck, ripping her collar as she did so.

Startled by this unexpected show of spirit, the man released his grip on both the girls.

"Constable, go and do some reading. Find out for yourself exactly what is going on in this world." As the man opened his mouth to speak, Nellie continued. "Better still, attend some of the meetings each week at the library. Listen to what the speakers have to say about what is happening to our world at the moment."

"Oh, aye?" The constable, beginning to recover, pulled out his baton. He began to slap it onto his palm, a meaningful look of menace on his face.

An intimidation tactic, if ever there was one, Nellie decided. She braced herself for battle.

Penny had begun to eye the man in consternation. He returned the look, and leered at her as though he was enjoying himself.

"The library, is it? A nest of dissenters–provocateurs against King and Country. Well, we'll see about that. We'll be shutting them down right enough, before y'can say 'Jack Robinson'!"

"*Fool*" Nellie, beside herself with fury, slapped the man's face, hard enough to make him blink in surprise. Just for a moment, he drew back.

Penny, in horror, shrieked "*Nellie*, no!"

Too late. Recovering himself, the constable, red of face, teeth bared and eyes aflame, raised his baton and brought it down, hard, on Nellie's shoulder.

She slumped down onto the pavement, with Penny wailing and kneeling beside her, just as the tram, horses snorting, arrived at the stop.

And Pa stepped out.

They were just over an hour at the police station. There were the usual flummery of exchanges: "He said," "She did," "I did *not* ..."

Apologies were demanded, and refused with an angry snort by Nellie.

Pa, having examined his daughter's sore shoulder, and deciding that nothing was actually broken, grudgingly supplied the desired apology.

Penny turned out to be something of a peacemaker.

"We are so sorry that things turned nasty. It's just that we had so enjoyed our evening and the constable"–here she turned to him with a winning smile–"misunderstood our, um … enthusiasm."

Nellie, rubbing her sore shoulder, snorted once more in derision. At which Penny and Pa automatically coughed in perfect unison, then smiled at one another. "*Snap!*" Obviously, their minds were in tune, something that Nellie did *not* appreciate.

Forms were filled out, signed and counter-signed by another constable who was rather more sympathetic than the first.

Eventually, and still fuming angrily, Nellie grudgingly allowed Pa and Penny to urge her out of the station.

They were followed by a parting shot from the offending constable. "Don't you let me find you coming this way again. I shan't forget yer faces, neither of you. Just remember that!"

Pa turned towards the man with a reproachful look. "Constable, I think that enough has been said and done tonight. These are two perfectly respectable young women, and if I hear of them being accosted again in like manner, there will be a complaint laid against you to the authorities." Then, with a dignified bow, and taking the pair of them, one on each arm, they left.

The constable, glowering furiously, slammed the door behind them–but not before they had heard some smothered laughter from the two other constables inside.

"Well." Pa sighed, watching the last tram as it disappeared around a distant corner. "Now we'll have to walk. Yer mams were both worried at the lateness of the pair of you as it was. That's why I'm here. Aye, well, we'll just have to make the best of it on Shank's pony."

Tired as he was, he set off at a brisk pace, with Penny trotting beside him. Nellie suddenly realised, now that the rush of angry adrenaline had left her, that she was absolutely exhausted.

Convinced, however, that her anger had been more than justified, she set her face to the growing cold and, shivering, followed resolutely in the wake of the other two.

*   *   *

"Will y'thank your Pa for me, Lovie, fer bringing home my Penny on Saturday, late as it was?"

With a twinkle in her eye, her hands busy at the loom, Alice raised her voice above the insistent clattering of the machines.

Nellie, still rankling from the scolding she had got from Mam two nights ago, pulled a face. Then, relenting, she smiled.

"Aye, well, you're welcome Alice. I heard all about it when we got home. Mam said she'd been that worried about how late we were. She sent Pa off in search of us.

"It was *such* an interesting talk, y'know. I expect Penny told you all about it. How we were all questioning the speaker afterwards, and us taking notes and ..."

"Aye, and how you two managed t'get on the wrong side of the law and all!"

The words were sharp, but the smile was warm. Nellie smiled back, and for the rest of the morning the two women worked in companionable silence, a silence broken only by the constant *clickety-clack* of the looms as they seized upon the wool that was being fed into them and turning it, by dint of warp and weft into massive sheets of material. The material would then be sent off to the tailors and dressmakers who, in turn, would craft the clothing for which it was intended.

The women working at the mill could not help but notice how the wool had been dyed a deep khaki–the colour of the army uniforms. It was a sobering thought to them, especially those with men at the Front. And there were many.

How many of these men–most of them so very young–would return home alive and whole? How many would be buried forever in a foreign soil, and, worst of all, how many would come limping home, minus a leg or an arm–blind, deaf or even deranged?

And then there would be those, mad of eye, twitching, jerking and jabbering from having inhaled the enemy gas.

Many of these casualties of an inhuman war, were already to be seen in the villages, towns and cities of the United Kingdom and her allies.

No, it could hardly be borne, the pain of these thoughts. Better to focus, fingers flying, on the work at hand. Warp and weft, weft and warp.

CHAPTER SEVEN
Sally Awakes

"Y're not going out there again, lass."

Mam, hands on hips shook her head in disbelief.

"Yes, of course, Mam. We're learning so much."

"Ha! Learning is it? More like learning to get on the wrong side of the law if you ask me."

Sally, slumped at the table, straightened up and nodded, seemingly in agreement. Nellie, noticing this, smiled to herself. The nighttime chats between the sisters, though somewhat one-sided, had recently resumed, and Nellie had begun to hope for some improvement. Here, she thought, was another small sign of hope.

Calmly, she rose from the table. Setting her plate and cup on the draining board, she began to run the cold water from the tap into the sink. The hot water was already bubbling on the stovetop.

Scooping up the soda crystals from the pot at the side of the sink, she dropped them into the water and began to swish at them with her hands, helping them to dissolve.

As she reached for the heated water, though, Mam intervened. She had not finished yet. Moving swiftly between Nellie and the stove, she barred her daughter's access.

"Mam?"

"Y're not getting out of here 'til you hearken to me, lass!"

"I'll do the dishes, Mam, then we can talk."

Reluctantly, her mother moved to one side, allowing Nellie to reach for the water and pour it into the sink.

Quickly, she cleaned and rinsed, placing the clean pots onto the draining board. Then, wiping her hands on the tea towel, she sat back down at the kitchen table and indicated, with a nod of her head, for her mother to join her.

Seating herself opposite, Mam sighed. Shaking her head, she said, "My, you've grown up, my lass, without me scarcely noticing it."

"Well,"–Nellie glanced toward Sally–"you've had other things on your mind, Mam, but, what is it you want to say?"

She reached across the table and gently squeezed her mother's hand. This proved to be too much for Mam. The tears began to flow, and she tightened her grip on this offered hand.

"Ach, lass. I've lost our George and our Will. I've lost our Sal, poor lamb."

The tears were now coursing down her cheeks and Nellie noticed again how worn she looked, how thin and tired. She folded her other hand on to her mother's.

From the corner of her eye, she noticed another change in Sally. Her sister had begun to lean forward, and she was listening intently to the conversation.

"Mam, you've not lost me," Nellie said.

This remark was, astonishingly, echoed by Sally's "Aye, you've not lost me, neither."

This was said in a voice that was scarcely above a whisper, but both women at the table turned, open-mouthed. Together, they looked towards the corner where Sally, formerly sitting, was now standing.

"Sal? My Sal?"

Nellie watched intently as, wiping her face with her apron, Mam started the few steps towards her other daughter. Reaching out her arms, she pulled Sally to her. Needing no further encouragement, Sally nestled into her mother's warm embrace.

Giving them a moment for this tremendous and unexpected union, Nellie, biting her lip in order to hold back tears of her own, now rose. Crossing over to them, she wrapped her arms around the pair.

"God bless you, Sal. Oh, God bless you!" Nellie could think of nothing more to say, and the three of them were still standing there, hugging, laughing and weeping all at one and the same time, when several moments later, Pa came through the door.

"Eee, but its parky out there," he began, but then stopped. He rubbed his eyes as though unable to believe what it was he was seeing.

The next moment, he had joined the others in their joyful embrace.

"Eee, lass, my wee lass! Art back among us then? Really back?"

Soon, they were sitting around the table, Sally, somewhat dazed at her own sudden return to present reality, and Nellie making tea.

Serving the tea, Nellie apologised. "I must go. I've missed the tram and I'll have to wait for the next. Penny will be out there on the other side of town. She'll be getting cold, and wondering what might have happened to me. I can hardly wait to tell her our good news."

"Of course y'must go. 'T'isn't right to leave the lass standing in the cold and all alone."

Pa was on his feet and helping Nellie into her coat. "D'you really have to go on to the meeting, though, lass?"

He watched as Nellie wound her scarf around her head and neck. Pulling on her gloves and grabbing for her bag, she made for the door.

"Yes, I really must. This is a very special meeting, and we promised ourselves we wouldn't miss it for the world."

Seeing the look on her mother's face she added, "Oh, Mam. Of course it's not as important as our Sal, but it *is* important. We'll come straight home as soon as it's done. No more lingering, I promise."

Swiftly, she moved to the table, giving both her mam and Sally a final kiss.

Whispering into Sally's ear, she murmured, "Welcome back, my lovie. I knew you'd make it back to us one day."

Turning at the door as she left, she blew a final kiss toward her gathered family. Once outside, she fairly flew down the street, grinning from ear to ear.

CHAPTER EIGHT

"Urgently Required"

The two girls were now waiting at the tram stop. It was cold. With scarves wound tightly around their throats, they shivered as they waited, the pair of them stomping from foot to foot.

"Brr ... but it's getting right parky now!" Penny said as she clapped her arms around her shoulders.

Nellie smiled. "I'll be glad to get home tonight."

"Aye, our Nell, I'm sure. What a miracle it is–about Sally, I mean. Y'were right brave to come out to the meeting on this night."

Nellie, detecting the slightest hint of criticism in her friend's tone, smiled.

"Well, I could hardly leave you waiting at the stop, wondering what might have happened to me, especially as it gets dark so early now and you never know who might come along. Some ignorant sort, perhaps, who would think that a woman alone is fair game."

Penny, recognizing the reference to the constable, smiled, and briefly reached out to touch Nellie's arm. "Aye, y're a good friend, our Nellie. I'll say that for you." She giggled. "Mind you, it could have been our very own friendly policeman that come around. I would have been quite safe with *him*."

Nellie snorted, and the pair of them collapsed in giggles for a moment. Then Penny's brow furrowed in thought.

"Do y'not think it a miracle, though, about Sally?"

"Nay," Nellie responded, and then added slowly, thoughtfully, "at least, I've been watching her for some time now, and thinking that something like this might be coming ..."

"Oh?" Penny's eyebrows were raised, inviting more revelation.

Well, y'see, we've always talked in bed at night, ever since we were small. But for ages–well, since, you know, this happened–she's not seemed to be listening."

"Aye." Again, Penny reached out with a sympathetic touch.

"But, oh, in perhaps the last six weeks or so, I've sensed a change in her. Except for just once, when she murmured my name, she's not answered me in *words*, nothing like that, but ..."

She broke off, gathering her thoughts. There was a moment of silence, but just as Penny opened her mouth to speak, Nellie continued.

"Yes, that's it! She has been giving me a listening silence. Different than before. Not exactly verbal mind, as I've said, but she has been *there* for me. I've been feeling her as being present instead of being far away in another land ..."

Gently, Penny handed her a clean handkerchief from her handbag. This, to wipe the tears that were now trickling, unheeded, down Nellie's cheeks as the enormity of what had happened had only now truly hit her.

"Oh, ta love." She blew hard into the flimsy material–lacy, pretty and so *very* Penny.

"I'll wash and iron it and bring it back tomorrow."

"Nay, no rush." Penny smiled. "But talking of tomorrow, we should meet and talk about this." She held up a copy of the poster that everyone at tonight's meeting had received.

There, in bold capitals, was the headline:

URGENTLY REQUIRED

Under that, a picture of three women, aproned and capped. Beneath this was printed:

VAD personnel urgently needed at the Front. Nurses, nursing aides, kitchen maids, ward maids and ambulance drivers.

Reading between the lines, the girls gathered that things were not going so well over there. Calls were now constantly coming from the fighting Front. More men were needed. How many had died, or been maimed beyond measure? Nellie wondered. She shivered–and not just from the cold, as she thought of her two brothers, currently in the thick of it. And what, she wondered, might also be happening to these volunteer support personnel? Were they not in grave danger, too?

The sound of the tram arriving reached the two friends, then, and gratefully, they clambered aboard.

CHAPTER NINE

To Go, or Not to Go?

A week later the small group sitting around the table at 87 Nanton Street–Mam, Pa, Alice, Nell and Penny–had reached a break in their earnest discussions. Even Sally, sitting a little apart, had been listening to the various argumentations from all sides, her eyes flitting back and forth between the speakers.

Now, taking advantage of the pause, she spoke up for the first time. "Shall us put the kettle on then, Mam? Make us another cup o' tea?"

Instantly, the worried frown disappeared from Mam's face. Beaming at the daughter she had until recently thought lost to her forever, she replied,"Aye, lovie. You do that then, my lass." As Sally rose, moving towards the sink, her mam beamed at the others around the table. "The brew that sorts all of our problems, eh?"

Encouraged by the changed momentum, everyone relaxed. Smiling and nodding in agreement, Alice continued in what had been the thrust of her argument. "After all, they'll be living at home for the first three months or so and, thanks to the kind offer from Sir Richard, our household incomes will not be suffering too much because of the absence of our girls."

The girls in question–Nell and Penny–exchanged somewhat derisive glances. After all, Hoyle's offer was mostly to his own advantage–Pa and Alice would have extra shifts at the mill and, also, there was now the distinct possibility that, with Sally's improving health, Mam might soon be able to take up a shift or two.

Penny, of course, had not been employed at the mill, so the loss was just of Nell. The only worry that both young women shared was the fact that there would be an extra burden of work laid upon the backs of their respective parents. So, if they took up the opportunity to go to the Front as volunteers, who knew how long this war would last ...

Feelings of guilt now mingled with their natural, youthful pleasure at the thought of the exciting new horizons opening before them.

Pa, sensing this, reached for the hand of each one of the pair and, taking them into his own strong, calloused hands, he reassured them. "Of *course* y'must go, young lasses. Our lads at the Front are in need of you."

Turning and nodding at the two mothers, he added, "And it'll be a great opportunity to see the world, how the other half lives. Who knows what other opportunities might be opened to you from a start like this?"

The kettle was now boiling, and Sally made the tea, serving it with a shy smile at the attending gathering.

Tea finished, Mam rose and stretched before settling in to her familiar organising bustle.

CHAPTER TEN

On the Move

Really, the fact that Robert Hoyle had been wounded in battle, was a piece of luck–at least for the two friends.

His injuries were not life-threatening, but it would mean that he would have both a limp, and a scar across his face that considerably diminished his boyish charms.

Between them, Vivienne Marchmont–the Lady in Blue and now Mrs. Robert Hoyle–and Charlotte, his distraught mother, had managed to persuade Sir Richard that Robert should be cared for at home during the period of his convalescence.

Sir Richard, eager to give the best care to his son, had not been difficult to persuade, and though initially, Robert was the sole patient in the large house, as more and more wounded men, some most grievously, had begun returning to Eldenfield and its environs, it soon became obvious that more help was needed.

And so, after applying to the Red Cross headquarters in London, Pembridge House, home to the Hoyle family, was pronounced to be suitable for use as a convalescent hospital.

A resident doctor was sent in, and a small team of trained nurses dispatched up to Eldenfield. These constituted the nucleus of the team that would be treating the returning maimed and dying men from the Front.

As the flood of these returnees steadily increased, it became more and more obvious that further help was needed in order to cope with the demand.

The supply of professionally trained medical aid was soon stretched to the limit. Many of these were working in the field hospitals at the Front, caring for the men who could not yet be moved.

As soon as it became feasible for these wounded to travel, they were packed into carts, ambulances, trains and boats, returning in droves to the British Isles.

By the time that Nell and Penny had been attracted by the poster advertisements, the situation had escalated from crisis to near catastrophic proportions and, so, the young women's applications had been seized upon with alacrity.

And now, as Alice had pointed out, the pair were to be trained locally for at least three months, and in the meantime, could continue to live at home. A situation that both Alice, and Bill and Jessie Parkin considered to be satisfactory.

During their training period, they would be engaged in the most basic of domestic duties. They would be scrubbing floors, washing blood-stained bedding, emptying slops and holding still the stumps–all that was left of the legs of poor, screaming men–as the nurses re-dressed their still-painful wounds.

Many of the young women were from the middle classes and had been sheltered and cosseted all of their lives. Brought up as "gentlewomen" they had never had to wash a cup and saucer, let alone hold down these bleeding men, and many of them fainted at the sights, sounds, and odours they had to deal with. These women would have to be revived, as the nurses rolled their eyes in impatient disgust.

No one, however, could complain about this kind of behaviour with regard to Nell, Penny or the other working-class young women who could be spared from mill work by their families. There were no complaints from them, as they rolled up their sleeves and set themselves to the work at hand.

The one difficulty that they shared with their middle-class co-workers, was that, being unmarried, they were not familiar with the whole, ungarnished male anatomy being presented to them.

Even those with brothers hitherto had had to guess at what lay beneath the concealing outer garments of the average grown male.

After the first shock, however, of encountering the nether regions of their suffering patients, they soon took such matters in stride.

Almost the worst thing to be endured were the working hours demanded of them. Nellie and Penny were up at 5 a.m. every morning. "Why," Mam had declared, "ye might as well be working at t'mill." This was said with pride, however, and the girls knew it.

Then, there was the catching of the early tram to the other side of Eldenfield. Followed by a trudge up the long, winding driveway to Pembridge House.

After that, it was life on the run. So many men were arriving almost daily now. "What is going on over there at the Front?" people asked in horrified wonder.

Nearly the whole of the once elegantly kept lawns of Pembridge House were now covered in canvas tents. This, to hold the overflow of patients.

Finally, it was home time and the last tram of the evening. Bed perhaps by ten, sometimes eleven at night. Sore, aching feet propped up on the bed and a candle lit on the side table. Then, the reading of homework would begin.

Up again at five a.m., and the whole rigmarole would begin again. At the end of this, though, they would have their certificates in basic first-aid and "Home Economics".

If successful in these, and with a good report from their superiors, they would be ready for the next step: a transfer to the Red Cross-run London General Hospital, in the slums of Camberwell Green, South London.

Following a few months there, and surviving the even more hectic pace, they would, with any luck, finally have qualified for acceptance to one of the many field hospitals at the Front. An exciting prospect, especially as they would now be being paid a small salary.

CHAPTER ELEVEN

To the Front

January 21, 1915

Dear Diary,

Well, here we are at last, at the Front.

Firstly, I have to jot down a big "thank you" to Alice, and Penny joins me in this, for having thought of presenting us such a roomy set of diaries for setting down our "adventures" as you call them.

Of course, we will be writing home, but we have been warned, as we always suspected from the tone of George's and now Will's letters, that what can be said in them must be very restricted. It will be the censor's big black pencil, else.

So, you will all have to wait for our first leave before you can dip into our exciting (and I'm sure they will be) revelations. So, here they are, set down for you all to read once we get back.

Our crossing from Dover to Boulogne was choppy, and we both felt a sinking in our stomachs that wasn't just the alarming sight of the White Cliffs of Dover, receding into the distance.

Boulogne was rainy and muddy with people both coming and going–many of them wounded men on stretchers going home with their bevy of caretakers. All of them glad to be going on leave.

A group of British "Tommies" spotted us and, knowing we were coming to help their comrades at the field hospitals, broke into wild cheering as they passed us in their convoy. We could still hear their cheering even when they had turned the corner. It was very touching, and made us feel humble as we thought of the task ahead of us.

The main railway line from Boulogne to Paris runs through a line of hospitals, all set at some distance from one another, all with their own number. Our hospital, number 24, is set just outside the town of Étaples, and on our arrival we were told that we would be together, with just one other VAD sharing our accommodation. Her name is "Cilla," short for (she eventually told us) Priscilla.

The accommodation itself is fairly primitive–just a wood and canvas shanty, known they tell us, as an "Alwyn" hut.

There was no sign of Cilla at first, so we set about hanging our clothes on the nails hammered roughly into the wooden part of the walls.

The only patients left here at the moment, are those too weak or too maimed to be moved. Most of them we have been told will probably be dead quite soon, and so will never see home again.

When we were told this, I found myself tearing up–thinking, of course, of George and Will. I noticed that Penny was like to cry as well, but we were both interrupted by Head Nurse Haines (a battleaxe, if ever there was one). "That's enough you two–if you're going to cry every time a man dies you'll be of no use to us, and might as well return home right now!" we were told. So of course we sniffed heartily, chorused "Yes, Nurse Haines" and promised to do better.

There was a rather doubting "Harumph" from Haines. She looked us up and down as though to say, "Look what the cat brought in now." Then rolling her eyes to the heavens, she strode off back to the wards.

As we were hastily finishing our unpacking, and preparing to follow Haines across to the lines of tents that constitute the wards, a rather austere young woman with a plain, round face entered the hut and introduced herself as our roommate, Cilla.

Holding out both arms to us, she smiled. Immediately, her face was transformed, and we all three warmed to one another.

Things were looking up. We'd found a friend.

Over the somewhat meagre supper, Cilla gave us the lie of the land. Most of what she described were situations that had already been explained to us during the course of our further training session at the London General in Camberwell.

She had had enough experience during the course of her three-month stint here that she was able to fill in the gaps quite handily. Most of what she told us wasn't pretty.

At Camberwell, we had learned the basics of recognising and dealing with fractures and loss of blood. We had learned, in short, how to deal with the things we could manage, and how to recognise those things that were beyond us, and which should be attended to by the professionals.

We soon found out, as Cilla warned us, that far from falling on us with cries of gratitude, we were received at best with a grudging acceptance, at worst with *downright hostility. Those very professionals–doctors and nurses–whom we were supposed to provide with support, regarded us as untrained bodies–here merely to get in their way.*

*   *   *

April 5, 1916

Dear Diary,

The fighting doesn't let up. I often wonder what we are really fighting for. Penny and I often remember what we were talking about that so angered the policeman at the tram stop last year. I still think that what we were saying is valid. There is a cabal of people "in the know" who are ready to seize upon any opportunity that presents itself to them that will be to their own advantage.

They take the presence of the ordinary working people as fodder for their machinations and do not give a second thought to the pain and loss we might suffer. We are merely pawns in a vast game of chess.

Look at this war, for instance. No sooner had the trigger been pulled at Sarajevo, than a mad scramble was begun to reclaim the lands of Alsace, initially lost in the Franco-Prussian wars of 1870-1871.

And so it continues with our poor men–of all nations battling to their deaths. For what. For what?

Oh dear, if anyone sees this I'll probably be charged as a traitor. I'll change the subject ...

I've made a friend. His name is Harry–Harry Briggs. A nice man, studying philosophy at the University of London until he came here. He is working here as a stretcher-bearer, as he feels that this is more important at this time than his studies.

Like many of the other bearers and medics, he is a pacifist and refuses to fight. No cowards they, though. They risk their lives on a daily basis, as they dig the special trenches needed to bring the wounded safely from the Front to the field hospitals, all the time, under almost constant fire.

Here, they have a brief respite, and we give them something hot and comforting to drink–preferably soup when it's available, for they have little time in the heat of battle to either eat or sleep.

After this, and once their poor burdens are off-loaded, they must turn around and do the whole thing over again. And again ... and again ...

Harry and I clicked immediately.

Over the course of several of these hurried meetings, I found myself spilling my heart out to him, regarding my lost opportunity to get myself an education. Sensing a kindred soul, he was immediately sympathetic, and promised to find me some readings that I might find interesting.

"I have some spare in my knapsack," he said, "wrapped in rubber to keep out the rain and the mud."

We laughed together at that, and Penny, looking up from serving soup to another man, gave me a smile and a knowing wink.

*   *   *

August, 1916

Dear Diary,

Well, we've had a bit of a break. Not long enough, I'm afraid, to get back home to you all. Oh, I'm so looking forward to seeing you all again, and giving you all the news in person!

This won't be possible until we've finished up our year here. We are still so short of help. But, recognising that a group of us were really feeling the pressure, it was decided that we must have a break, in order to renew ourselves.

So, they sent us to a place behind the lines—an ancient château, where a group of nuns tended to us so very kindly, sharing their food with us, despite the severe shortages that everyone is experiencing these days.

We stayed for ten days and left feeling refreshed and ready for our own battles once more ...

The fighting goes on and on. It is heartbreaking, watching the endless arrival of stricken men. Every day, at regular intervals they come, accompanied by their weary bearers.

I find myself looking out for Harry. Sometimes he is among them, sometimes not. I find myself missing him. Which of course, is ridiculous.

Cilla is really very nice. She seems quite mature in her ways—what you, Mam, in one of your more romantic moments, would call "An old soul."

I noticed how well she seemed to get on with the nuns while we were at the château. They took to her, as well, and she and they chattered away in French. I wished that I had learned it. Though we have been in France for coming up to a year, we are just so very busy with our work. There is no time for anything else–except for my diary writing, of course!

Well, back to Cilla. Nothing seems to faze her. She deals with our extreme moments of rush and stress calmly and competently, ignoring the conflicting pleas from the medics ("Here nurse! Here, right now!"), and yet seems to end up satisfying everyone.

Penny and I admire her enormously, but she discourages our enthusiastic praise with a dismissive gesture, giving us one of her rare, warm smiles, indicating that we are not to feel hurt by her seemingly brushing us off.

The other day, we were working with a newly arrived group of badly injured men. I still find it so difficult to deal with someone holding fast to my hands, and then, right before me, gathering his last painful breath and dying right there and then. It seems so very unfair.

Anyway, there was this very young lad–couldn't have been more than seventeen. He was bleeding profusely, and Cilla, as she tried to staunch the flow, was getting covered in his blood. He was obviously about to die and began crying for his mam.

Without blinking an eyelid, Cilla, giving up her battle against the flow, held both his hands in hers and began to croon: "There, there, my lovely boy. Mama is here, Mama is here..."

The lad turned his head towards her and began to smile.

A medic, obviously harassed out of his wits, snarled at her, "Leave him, leave him be–you can do him no good now."

Then, as she continued to croon: "Leave him, I said– Goddammit, I need you here!"

Out of the blue, Nurse Haines appeared. Calmly, she touched Cilla's shoulder, murmuring, "Good girl," before hastening over to the medic to give him the help he needed.

Busy as I was myself. I looked back at Cilla and the boy. He was now quite dead, but with a smile still on his face. Cilla, unable to save his life, had given him the best help she could.

As I watched, she kissed her fingers, and then laid them gently on his forehead, before rising, wiping her hands, and moving on to the next young man in line.

I saw Nurse Haines' face soften, as she glanced up for a moment, regarding the young woman. It was then that I began to revise my previous opinion of our "battleaxe."

That night, in bed, Penny and I discussed this incident. Obviously, Nurse Haines had been through the mill. She knew, as we were now discovering, that the only possible way to survive this mindless slaughter was to remain calm and centred. To wearily put one foot in front of the other–and to just keep going.

As we fell into an exhausted slumber, already we could hear the sound of distant gunfire.

Another skirmish was underway.

CHAPTER TWELVE
Harry and Nellie

Early Autumn, 1916

It had begun to dawn on Nellie how, scarcely without knowing it, she had begun to rely on the sheer, kindly concern that she was receiving from Harry. A comradeship had developed between them, an easy friendliness that she now realised she treasured. It occurred to her that Harry responded in like manner. They had, in effect, become a "team."

In their snatched moments together, he would tell her some of the more amusing incidents that occurred during the course of his bearer duties. One day, as they sat together in a brief moment of respite, he related, half shocked, half amused, the story of Charlie...

He had come across the man, a Cockney soldier, hovering in disbelief over the dead body of a fallen comrade. "Pore Fred," he was exclaiming, over and over again. "Pore ole Fred. It oughter 'ave been me! It were no more'n a minute. I 'ad ter go fer a whiz. 'E moved over and 'is 'ead were against the place where mine 'ad been not a minute before. The bullet 'it 'im straight between the eyes."

Then, still shaking in disbelief "Pore 'ole Fred. 'E copped it, did'n 'e. Copped the bullet meant fer me ..."

While loading "Pore Fred" onto the stretcher, Harry had done his best to soothe the shaking Charlie. Then, with his fellow bearer sharing the burden, they had taken off along the narrow trench, dug especially for the purpose of shielding medics and bearers from the almost constant sniping from the other side.

Another time, as Harry arrived to collect yet another "crop" of dead and injured men, he had encountered a uniformed soldier, ambling casually alongside the trench. This, in full view of the enemy lines.

He had been delivering, it turned out, the eagerly awaited letters and parcels from home.

Harry, intrigued, had asked him if he wasn't afraid of getting shot.

"Oh, no," the man replied. "If I get shot today, it'll save me the trouble of getting shot tomorrow." And with that, he had continued cheerfully on his way.

Harry and Nellie had laughed heartily at the sheer insouciance of the soldier's attitude. But then, quite suddenly, Nellie had begun to cry.

Once having started, she just couldn't seem able to stop. Gently, Harry had put his arms around her, holding her tight.

"I know, I know," he had whispered in her ear. "It's all so awful–it's almost beyond bearing. But we must stay strong. For the sake of the men, we *must* stay strong."

Then, he had fumbled in his pockets, in search of an available handkerchief–eventually drawing forth a somewhat grubby article that could, possibly at one time, have been called a handkerchief.

Apologetically, he fumbled again with the article, in due time finding a middling clean spot that, equally apologetically, he spat upon, then used to dab at her red, tear-stained face.

Strangely, rather than being repelled by these somewhat primitive ministrations, Nellie felt enormously comforted. Sighing, she allowed herself to relax further into his embrace.

Handing her the by now soggy piece of material, he kissed her very gently on the forehead, before letting her go.

"Thank you," she said, somewhat tremulously.

He had smiled. "Any time," he replied. "I'm here for you anytime." Then abruptly, he turned and headed back, down to the trench and into the face of danger.

That night, as Penny and she lay whispering their usual pre-sleep summations of the day, Nellie told her of this incident.

Immediately, Penny was wide awake and hugely excited. "I knew it!" she said, thumping her friend's arm in her glee. "I *knew* you two were going to fall in love, almost from the moment you first clapped eyes on one another!"

Laughing, Nellie attempted to refute all suggestions of the idea of falling in love. But then there came a soft chuckle from Cilla's bed.

"I'm sorry," she apologised. "I didn't mean to eavesdrop, but really Nellie, we *all* could see what was going to happen with you two. Almost from the start. You seem to be the last one to know it, but believe me, anyone can see how suited you are to one another. Follow your heart young lady, follow your heart."

With that, she turned on her side and, still chuckling, settled herself for sleep.

With a final, whispered *"See?"* Penny also turned, snuggling into her pillow with a contented sigh.

As the gentle snoring began from the other two beds, Nellie lay awake. The implications of all that had happened began to dawn on her, and with it, the unwelcome feelings of anxiety with regard to Harry's safety.

First George, then Will, and now Harry. Could she bear any further emotional investment in these oh-so vulnerable young men?

Lying there, listening to the usual nightly sounds of skirmishing in the distance, she realised that she could. She had no choice. She loved Harry with all her heart, and there was an end to it.

She would bear whatever loss might come to her. Just as all of the other women would. The mothers, sisters, wives and daughters.

These were among the casualties of this dreadful, stupid war, just as much as were their dead and maimed men.

As, eventually, she began to drift into sleep, another thought came to her. Why was that soldier–the one delivering the letters and parcels--why was he allowed to go on without some sniper shooting him down?

With a shiver, the thought came to her that the young German soldiers had recognised what his actions represented. They, too, longed for the comfort of news and "goodies" from home.

The sight of these deliveries must have been to them a sign of their shared humanity. Just for a moment, this man had been spared.

Tomorrow might well be a different story ...

CHAPTER THIRTEEN

Good News, Bad News

April 1917

"Good news! Good news!" The three young women were hugging and laughing in their tent. The news had just arrived that, finally, and after much discussion, objections had all been overcome. The Americans were joining them in the war effort.

"Phew–and about time, too!" Breathless, Penny plonked herself down on her bed. "We seem to have been hanging by a thread for so long now."

"Aye. Things turned really bad last year. Remember that time when they told us to be prepared to abandon our spot here? What a palaver that would have been." Nellie shook her head as she spoke.

"Well"–Cilla was nodding in satisfaction "–though their politicians have been reluctant to let them go, it would seem from what I've heard that the men themselves are raring to join us in the fight. Also, it just might be the end of American isolationist thinking. Though," she continued, wrinkling her brow in thought, "one can understand the reason *why* their country wants so badly to stand alone."

"Oh?" Nellie, head cocked on one side, was curious. Both she and Penny were ardent admirers of this educated roommate of theirs, and listened to her opinions with respect.

Cilla, smiling fondly at the younger pair, continued: "Well, they had, of course, to fight hard enough to become an independent nation in the first place. But now"–she sighed–"this is a *world* war, like it or not."

By now, exhausted by their working day, the burst of joyous energy had evaporated, and all three of the women were lying on their beds.

"Oh, I could stay lying here for *ev*–" Nellie began. She was cut short by the sound of the bugle.

Everyone exchanged rueful glances. Then "To arms!" Cilla cried. "*To arms!*" came the response from the other two. Heaving themselves up from their beds, they prepared to meet the incoming wounded.

*　　*　　*

"We're going on leave – we're going on leave!"

Penny was hugging herself in delight. Nell laughed. "Aye, we are that," she said, reverting to the broad vernacular of Eldenfield.

The pair were taking a break from the wards. This, with the permission of Nurse Haines. "Things are quiet enough for the moment," she had said.

One never knew, of course, when the next "push" on the part of the troops would bring the stretcher-bearers, carrying load after load of wounded men. They were moving as fast as was feasible in the deep trenches. At least in August there was comparatively little actual mud.

So, sitting on two upturned, empty supply boxes, and basking in the August sunshine, the two friends were sipping tea. It was rather an insipid beverage–more hot water than tea, and minus either milk, or sugar. Supplies were running low, and what there were, were of course, given to the men.

Delighted as they were with themselves, however, the pair sipped with enjoyment, as they chatted merrily on, making their plans for the journey.

"It's been just over a year and a half. Oh, it'll be so good to see me mam again." Penny's brow clouded for a moment, thinking of what her mother must be feeling by now.

Seeing this touch of melancholy in her friend, Nellie stretched out a sympathetic hand, holding her wrist in a warm grasp.

Much had happened in the last few months. The news, as always, had been desperately slow in filtering through, and much had been blotted out by the censor's strokes of the pen.

Harry had been more than helpful though, bringing the snippets of gossip and news that filtered down through the lines.

Gareth Hodge had achieved his heart's desire and, young as he was, had been accepted to work with the multitude of horses employed as "Engines of War."

In some cases, early in the war, these were ridden by the officers and men of the elite cavalry units. But, as time went on, the use of the heavy guns of war made the cavalry redundant.

Most of the horses were now employed for the purpose of hauling heavy equipment–everything from the great guns, to ambulances and supply trucks.

As such, they were fair game for coming under enemy fire, and were perishing in the thousands.

It was not an unusual sight to find the sad remains of what had once been a fine piece of horseflesh, lying in its own blood. The dead face, once so noble, now with lips drawn back in the rictus of an agonised death.

The flies, so many of these, would be buzzing busily about what had been left by the rats. No compassionate stretcher-bearers, no medics for the horses. They had, of necessity, been left where they were lying.

Nature would take its course ...

Both Nell, and Gareth's sister Penny, could imagine how this reality must have put an end to his romantic vision of working with his much-loved animals.

He had, apparently, after the first shock of realisation had passed, set to with a will to do his best to care for and protect his charges.

Eventually, though, an incident had occurred that had broken his spirit. The news of his fate had come down to Penny through the grapevine, long before her mother's anguished letter had reached her.

Harry, grave of face, had taken her hands in his, and told what he knew of her young brother's fate.

Apparently, Gareth had been in sole charge of twenty stallions, these to be delivered down the line. All had been well, until they had reached the rickety gate of a now derelict farmhouse. Suddenly, a group of enemy planes–G17s and Albatross-had swept down from behind the clouds, firing furiously.

The horses had not stood a chance. In blind panic they charged the gate, their legs becoming entangled in the broken spars. And there they lay, while the bullets flew, hitting them in the stomach, the neck, the head, the eyes ...

The last that had been seen of Gareth was from behind, as, screaming his fury and pain and ignoring the flying bullets, he had ridden away into the distance, followed by just two of the surviving horses.

These, blind with panic as they were, knew only to follow the young man who loved them, and who had gained their trust.

Nothing had been seen of them since.

With Harry still holding her hands, Penny had wept, while Nell, shocked, had wrapped her arms around her friend, murmuring what comforting words and clucks she could muster.

Now, three weeks later, and with the happy thoughts of their coming leave, the pair sat on their makeshift seats, draining their cups, and turning their faces to the benediction of the August sun.

"I just can't *wait* to see home again!" This from Penny, while Nell gathered the teacups together, shaking out the dregs onto the earth, and then tamping them down with her foot.

"Aye, my mam says they are going hungry, though. She and others have been out gathering stinging nettles, y'know, to make nettle soup. And Pa says it's like going back to 1812–when the workers from the new slums had to sustain themselves with practically nothing but nettle soup."

Penny's eyes widened. "I'd not heard of that!" she exclaimed.

"Aye, the people of the countryside had come into the towns, flocking in to work at the new factories, and looking for the better life promised them by the owners."

Nellie fell silent for a moment, remembering her readings and the discussions with her father. She smiled fondly, thinking of those days when both she and he had thought her to be well on her way to scholarship.

"So," Penny broke into her thoughts, "how much better off do you think we are now? Me mam and your pa, and all of the others in Eldenfield–working their fingers to the bone, just to sustain a bare living for themselves."

Her tone was vehement, and Nellie couldn't help smiling at her fondly.

"Aye, well, I suppose we are a bit better off than they were in them ..." She paused to correct herself in mid-sentence "In *those* days, but we've a way to go yet," she added.

Penny giggled, and then, mischievously referring to Nell's grammatical self-correction; "I see all of *them* books what ..." here, she broke off, giggling again. "*Those* books *that* you've been reading and discussing with Harry have been doing you a bit of good."

Blushing, Nellie nodded in silent, if somewhat wistful agreement.

There had been no more tender moments recently between Harry and herself. Often, he seemed distracted, almost distant. Always polite, always kind, of course, but then he was that to everyone. She realised now with a frisson of shock, she wanted more from him.

Her face must have shown something of her feelings, for Penny now took her hands, saying softly, "He loves you, y'know. He truly does ..."

Before she could finish her sentence, however, Nellie had withdrawn into herself, shaking her head in negation of what was being said.

Before Penny could pursue the subject further, the bugle sounded. More wounded were on their way.

The frantic melee that always happened when yet another group of men arrived, took time to be converted into an orderly process. This time matters were made even worse by the fact that the stretchers, the men on them, and the bearers carrying them, had been under fire themselves.

The wounded men, unconscious, or groaning in pain, were lifted by the bearers as gently as possible onto the beds waiting for them.

The medics came to give their appraisal as to whom should be given priority, as far as surgery was concerned. The nurses and their aides scissored off the torn and bloody remnants of army uniforms.

Then, the wounds exposed, the work of cleansing, disinfecting and bandaging began.

Hours later, the bearers, having been fed and rested, gathered the stretchers and issue of clean blankets together, ready to make their way back to the lines.

A group of nurses and aides was clearing up the tattered remnants of army uniforms, ready for dispatch into the ovens. Another group, including Penny, was carrying the soiled blankets to be washed.

A young bearer approached this group, asking if they knew of a Nellie Parkin. Everyone pointed to Penny. Rather wearily, she nodded, saying "Yes?"

"I've been given a message for 'er. Miss. Me name's Joe. Can I speak to 'er?"

"Oh, I'm sorry, Joe, but she's in the operating tent at the moment. Can I help?"

Instantly, the others gathered around, bristling with curiosity. The topic of Nellie's stalled romance had been the subject of much speculation for several weeks now.

Unaccustomed as he was to being the centre of quite so much female interest, Joe shifted uncomfortably from foot to foot.

"Well, er ..." He gulped nervously, and a few of the nurses began to giggle. Now he clammed up entirely. His eyes bugging out of his head, he began desperately looking around for escape.

Remembering her own brother, and how he would tend to be embarrassed by unwanted female attention, Penny, tactfully aware of the poor boy's embarrassment, handed off her load of blankets to a couple of willing young women.

Turning to Joe, she took him aside, leading him by the elbow.

"Now," she said, as the others, deprived of their gossipy interest, moved off about their errands. "What is this message?"

As Joe still seemed doubtful about delivering the message to anyone not the designated person, she added, "I'm her best friend, have been for ages. We're from the same town."

That seemed to settle things for Joe. Fumbling in his pockets, he brought forth a crumpled piece of paper that had been hastily scribbled on with pencil.

His comrades, sounding impatient, were now calling, "Joe, get a move on, lad, or we'll not be back 'fore mornin'!"

Hastily, Joe thrust the message into Penny's outstretched fingers.

"Ta miss," he mumbled, and was gone.

Nellie could not have known, for he had said nothing to her, that Harry's feelings for her had been growing stronger each time that they had met.

But, looking around at the devastating evidence of man's inhumanity to man, he could not see any future for those who might survive this appalling, inhuman, war.

And, if he could not see a future for those around him, his fellow travellers, then also, he could see no point in pursuing an affair of the heart that, at any moment, could be undone by the merest fluke of a stray bullet.

So, he had said nothing.

"Damn him! *Damn the wretched man!*"

While Cilla and Penny sat, dumbstruck, on their beds, Nellie raged–furiously beating at her pillow as, it would seem, she would wish to be beating Harry, the object of her fury.

Penny and Cilla both knew better than to intervene. Not just yet at any rate.

The tirade continued, while the other two watched in sympathy, occasionally exchanging concerned glances with one another.

Cilla, having settled her charges for the night, had entered their sleeping quarters just as Penny was handing over Joe's note.

There had been a sudden, sharp intake of breath, as Nellie began reading the contents, and the two young women, looking at one another in foreboding, settled themselves on their beds to wait.

They did not have to wait for long. The note contained bad news–that was certain–and they had been expecting to comfort tears, but not *this*. Not such furious anger.

The rage had worn itself out soon enough, and the tears had begun.

Shaking her head in negation against the others, now moving as one to comfort, Nellie held up the note for them to read, before burying her head into the much abused pillow as silent tears ran down her face.

Sitting on Cilla's bed, they read the note:

My dear, dear girl,

I know that your feeling for me has grown over the last months, as mine has for you.

It is to this end, then, that I must say goodbye. I have put in to be moved down the line to a field hospital nearer to the main front. My reasoning for this move is, I am sure, something you will understand.

This terrible, inhuman war has taken away the usual reasons for living–love, happiness and the desire for scholarship that I know are things that we share.

All that is left is the daily battle to serve the poor men– victims of political self-interest, and the incompetence of self-important leaders who have no true knowledge of the science of warfare.

I am reminded here of the "Grand Old Duke of York," who, no doubt, lost most of his ten thousand men!

These are they who will dispatch their men, against an often better organised enemy and, when the inevitable slaughter ensues, will blithely send back for more men.

Enough of this "For God and glory" nonsense. It is nothing but a sham–a game of chess across the face of Europe and beyond, and we are the pawns.

Maybe, just maybe, if this mayhem ever ends, we might meet again. I know that you come from Eldenfield, and that I could make enquiries there, if we all survive.

For the time being, though, with us both being so heavily involved in the heart of this war, I can see no future for our friendship.

Forgive me, my dearest. Understand that I am broken-hearted regarding this move, but I truly cannot continue in this way. A clean break is for the best.

I wish you well, with all my heart.

Harry B. x

Silently, Penny and Cilla looked at one another, at first not knowing what to say.

The tears were already forming in Penny's eyes, ready to course down her cheeks. "I never would have thought he could be so cruel" she said, swiping furiously at the tears. "Never, never. He's just a-a-*fool*."

"No." As Penny rose, ready to move across to her friend, Cilla caught her arm, and she sat. "No, let her be–let her cry it out. I don't think," she added, "that he is either a fool or a cruel person. I think the poor man is in despair and that he needs help."

Both of the other two, wiping away the tears, now looked at Cilla with some hope. They had seen her in action so many times, and had grown to trust her compassionate wisdom. She truly was a remarkable person, someone in whom you could believe.

Slowly, Nellie sat up. Throwing her legs over the edge of the bed, she wiped her eyes and blew her nose. Then, heaving a great sigh of fresh breath into her lungs, she said softly, "Thank you, Cilla."

Reaching out to grasp the other's hand in both of her own, she continued. "You are so wise, Cilla, and so very kind." She glanced for a moment at Penny, who was nodding vigorously in agreement.

"I think"-Nellie furrowed her brow in thought-"it seems to me that I should spend this leave searching for Harry." Then, as Penny opened her mouth, ready to protest, she beat her to the punch. "*Yes*, Penny, I've got to find him. I've got to show him that we are together in this-that we can see it through."

"But your mam, your pa-and Sally. They must be so looking forward to seeing you again, and well, with George and Will still away ... no, you can't disappoint them. You can't."

Penny was visibly shocked and upset.

"You're both right." Cilla's calm voice broke into the mounting tension between the pair. Turning to Nellie, and gently extricating her hands from between the tightening grip, she reached out a hand to each of them.

"If you would take some advice?" Her voice rose in a question mark. Both girls nodded vigorously.

"I ... I have some contacts that might be of help." As the girls leaned forward in expectation, she hesitated, then said, "I've not spoken of this before, not to anyone here, except Nurse Haines."

Again she hesitated, and the girls, now thoroughly intrigued, were agog.

"Please, promise me that you won't speak of this to anyone."

Without a word, and after a quiet glance between them, the girls nodded.

I was ... I *am* a nun." Then, as two jaws dropped open, and two pairs of eyes widened in astonishment, she laughed.

"But-but-but ..." Two voices stuttered in unison.

The first to recover, Penny asked, "But, what happened? What did you do?"

Nellie nodded vigorously, her eyebrows raised in silent query.

Again, Cilla laughed. "Oh, there is nothing sinister to report." She smiled fondly at the two of them, as they looked relieved at this, then went on. "I attended a convent school and loved the place. I decided very early–too early as it turns out–that I wanted to join the sisters and become one with them.

"My mother had died when I was very young, but after my father and the Reverend Mother had discussed the matter thoroughly, it was decided that I would be accepted as a novice at the age of sixteen."

"And then you didn't like it after all?" This from Nellie.

"Oh no, not immediately. I loved the place, I loved the quiet prayerfulness of the daily routine, but ..." she paused in reflection.

"*BUT?*" This from both girls in unison. Then, from Penny, "But then you decided you didn't like the life after all?"

"No, it wasn't a sudden change, more of a dawning realisation that I wanted more. I wanted to *be* more. I wanted to engage with the world outside more, and I wanted to serve my fellow human beings more practically than just in prayer–important as that can be, of course."

"So you left? Just like that?" This from Penny, sounding as though this was something of an anti-climax, a descent from the exotic to the humdrum.

Again, Cilla laughed. She looked at the pair of them with great fondness.

"My point in telling you this is that the sisters, concerned for my welfare, introduced me to the Knights Templar of St. John–a Catholic organisation that, among other things, has a branch that specialises in finding those who have become lost in conflict".

By now, the two young women were beginning to understand the thrust of Cilla's confidences.

"So"–Nellie was excited now–"you think you can find out from them where Harry might be?"

"It might be simpler than that, Nellie. You see, there is often an exchange of information between the Templars and the Red Cross. In fact, that is how I came to be aware of the Red Cross services in the first place. I took the basic nurse training, and when the war began, there I was, ready to serve."

"Oh, my goodness!" This from Penny. "What an interesting life you've had so far, Cilla."

Once more, and shaking her head in amusement, Cilla laughed at the sweetly naïve comments from the pair of them. The laugh, however, was interrupted by a semi-stifled yawn.

"We can't stay up all night you know, my dears. And you must be at *least* as tired as I am".

"But …" This from an anxious-looking Nellie. "What did you mean, it might be simpler than that?"

"Why, it might be as simple as asking each group of bearers when they come in–*somebody* must know more about his whereabouts. He must have mentioned where he was intending to end up.

The main thing for the moment," she continued, "is for the pair of you to *go home*. Comfort your parents with your presence. It's been a long time since you were there, and they must be missing you very much–especially your mam, dear Penny, after what has happened to Gareth".

Penny nodded thoughtfully. "Aye, Cilla. Y'right there." She looked toward Nellie for confirmation.

"But, will you keep asking the bearers Cilla? Please?"

"Yes, Nellie, of course I will. And if there's nothing doing there by the time you get back, why, we'll start extending the search with both the Knights of St. John and the Red Cross. Promise!

"Now," she continued, "*bed* and *sleep*–else the morning will have come, and we'll be fit for nothing".

Obediently, the girls settled into their beds.

"G'night, Cilla."

"G'night, Cilla. Thank you."

"Goodnight, my dears. You have a long journey to be fit for tomorrow. Sleep well".

Quite soon, the tiny sleeping hut was quiet, save for the sound of gentle snoring from the two girls.

Cilla, however, lay wakefully, her eyes wide open, as she prayed for guidance.

CHAPTER FOURTEEN

Home

The journey from Étaples station into Boulogne, seemed comparatively dreary-this compared to the excitement they had experienced before, on their way into a brave new world.

The train was crowded with both locals-the women holding clucking hens, in baskets on their knees; the men smoking their pipes and chatting with their neighbours-and soldiers.

There were also, of course, the endless consignments of recovering wounded, bound like them for home.

There were many stops and starts along the way. During these pauses, conversation ceased, as people strained their ears, listening for a possible approaching attack.

Each time the engine started again with a roaring and puffing of smoke, and the train lurched into motion, there was a general sigh of relief. Nellie, as taut with nervous response as everyone else, realised yet again, how hard this war was on everyone.

Even if one escaped from being wounded, the drain on the nervous system was taking a mighty toll on people's lives.

Once again, she thought of Harry, and once again her feelings melted into sympathetic understanding-a far cry from the initial, furious anger she had felt while she was first reading his note.

Penny, watching her, smiled and reached out a hand to hers in a brief grip. Nellie smiling also, returned the grasp. What good friends they had become during the course of the last nearly two years. She smiled again, recalling the time-now seeming so long ago-when she had sat in Alice's kitchen, and had first heard mention of Penny's name.

The docks at Boulogne were crowded. A frenetic mass of people were milling around in seeming disorder. Officials were shouting out directions, busily trying to create some semblance of order. Most people just kept on pushing and shoving until they reached their desired goal.

Disciplined groups of Tommies were being marshalled by the stentorian tones of their various sergeant majors. Her heart gave a lurch, as she thought of what was ahead of them.

And, of course, there were the wounded, headed for home. Both the girls noticed several of these young soldiers, glancing askance as they made way for the stretchers bearing legless, or armless or blinded men.

Now, Nellie thought, the reality is beginning to dawn. This is going to be so much more than the adventure they might have been thinking it to be.

One of the young men, seeing that the girls were looking in his direction, and noticing their Red Cross uniforms, straightened up and gave them a smart salute.

Touched by this gesture, both girls smiled, gracefully nodding their thanks.

There had been no alert out today for any submarine activity in the channel, and when, standing on the deck, they watched the approaching white cliffs-not so white today in the drizzling rain-the girls joined in with the cheer that went up at the sight.

Next came the train journey to London, a change there for Leeds, where they would change yet again for Eldenfield.

It was nearly ten in the evening, before the now thoroughly exhausted young women were woken from a restless dozing by the Station Master's cry of "Eldenfield! Eldenfield Junction!"

Scrambling to their feet and fumbling their luggage from the overhead racks, Penny and Nell opened the door and stepped wearily onto the platform.

And there was Pa, a huge, beaming smile on his face, waiting for them.

No time for hugs and kisses yet–there was the last tram to catch.

Once boarded, the happy greetings began. "Eee, lassies, it's so good to see the pair of thee back home. Yer mams, both of them, will be that glad for thee!" To Nellie he said, "Yer mam's made a big stew. Don't ask me where she managed to find all that she needed for it, times being hard just now."

For a brief moment, his brow furrowed in displeasure at the state of things, but then, looking at them, he beamed once more.

Holding out his hands, first to one, then the other, he briefly held each face, looking at each of them in turn, as if hardly believing they were really there.

"Eee, but I'm that glad." He repeated softly, "That glad."

A short walk from the stop, and they were outside number 85 Nanton Street. The door flew open before Pa could even reach for the latch, and what seemed like a multitude of hands were reaching, touching, holding them in a huge, familial embrace.

Tears, smiles and exclamations of joy were the order of the day, as the combined members of the Parkin and Hodge families, united in their happiness, welcomed two of their members back into the fold.

Much later, stuffed with Mam's stew–oh, how good home cooking was–Penny and Nell were coming almost to the end of recounting their saga. Their "adventures" as the family insisted on calling them. Nellie noticed the glances that Izzie was giving her sister–glances full of longing. She was obviously dying to ask Penny if there was news of Gary. Nellie noticed, too, with sympathy, that Penny was feeling uneasy, knowing that she would soon have to tell her mother and sister that no, there was no news.

Seeing that Penny was avoiding her pleading glances, Izzie at last burst forth with the dreaded question. "Have you any news of our Gary?"

In the silence that followed, the eyes of the entire gathering were upon them. Nellie's heart clenched, as she saw the look of longing in Alice's eyes, wavering between hope and sadness.

Both young women, attuned to each other as they had become, glanced at one another, as though to say, "*What can we tell them?*"

Then, with a nod from Nell, Penny spoke up.

Taking her mother's hands in hers, she said, "Mam, we don't know, we just don't know ..." Then, as her mother's face crumpled, she added, "But Nellie and me–and I," she corrected herself as Nellie smiled, "we've been talking to some of the lads, the stretcher-bearers at the field hospitals. They're the ones that bring us all the gossip and news from down the line..."

Here, she gave a quick glance at Nellie, remembering Cilla's words of hope regarding Harry, and Nellie nodded in acknowledgement. Penny continued. "If anything is heard, *anything* at all, you can be sure that we will hear about it, Mam, you can be sure ..."

Alice nodded, but her face was drawn and sad, and Nellie thought yet again, of how hard life was for these people left at home, to wonder and hope, and wonder again.

All that evening, following the initial hugs of greeting, Sally had kept herself in the background. Hovering between stove, sink, and table, she had been making an excellent job of helping the two mothers as they served up the food and cleared away the plates.

Now, having boiled the kettle, she was busily making tea, bringing over the steaming cups to the others, as they continued their discussions at the table.

After she had made sure that everyone had tea, she sat down beside Alice. Shyly, briefly touching the older woman's arm, she said, "Eee, tha' should not grieve, Mrs. Alice. They'll find your Gareth safe and sound. I know it, but not until this war is over and done with–right at the end, you'll see".

She sounded so very positive, that Nellie, astonished, looked around at the others to see how they were receiving this information, so confidently given.

She was further astonished to see that they were receiving it very well. Mam and Pa were exchanging glances, and looking proudly satisfied. Izzie was nodding and smiling, and Alice herself looked, if not exactly happy, at least rather relieved.

Nell and Penny exchanged glances of their own that were the equivalent of a puzzled shrug.

There was a mystery here, and Nellie made a mental note to find out, at the earliest opportunity, what that mystery might be.

CHAPTER FIFTEEN
Bad News

September 1917

"It's going to be a lovely day, our Nell. Why don't you lassies take the tram out to the woods on t'other side of town? I know, Nellie, you've always loved it out there."

Mam, bustling round the kitchen on a fine Saturday morning, and readying herself for work, beamed fondly at her daughters. "There's no point in wasting such a lovely day. Y'never know when there might be another at this time o' the year."

A shadow crossed her face as she continued. "Aye, and you and young Penny will be leaving afore the end of the month. Back to that ... to that dreadful place."

Her mouth quivered for a moment with this, and Nellie moved to comfort her. Her mother, though, pulled herself together, lifting her chin. "Aye, well", she went on, "yer Pa is right–we've all got to do our bit while this war goes on!

"Besides, ye'll be able to keep a closer eye on what's happening with our boys." Again, there was a slight quiver, and again, she pulled herself up. "Ye never know who you might meet, what knows something about our George and our Will."

Seeing Nellie's expression, she added hastily, "Oh, lovie, I know it must be like looking for a needle in a haystack, but y'never know, and besides, there's Penny's Gareth and"–wrapping her arms around Nellie in a quick hug–"there's your Harry."

She beamed encouragingly at her daughter, before saying, "Oh, there goes the siren–I'll be late!" Then, she was out the door, and gone.

Nellie had been hoping to find out her mother's opinion regarding Sally's certainty of Gareth's safe return. Now, she was left to reflect bitterly at how all of their lives were ruled–by the siren, or by the bugle's call, by the mill boss or the general, rallying his officers and privates. It was all the same. People were merely pawns, fodder to be worked or shot at until the day of their death.

"Nellie?" Sally's soft voice interrupted this rather bleak reverie. "Nellie, will ye be off then, with our Penny?" As Sally shifted over to make more room for her at the table, Nellie wondered if, perhaps, this might be the time to ask her sister to satisfy her curiosity.

But then, as the sun, shifting its position, peered through the kitchen window, her mood brightened. Mam was right, it *was* going to be a lovely day.

"Yes, Sal, I think we will be going out, Penny and me. Will you come with us? That would be nice."

This was asked without much hope. Apart from doing the marketing, Sally, it would seem, never went anywhere. She seemed to be perfectly content in her role of domestic helper, having no desire for doing anything else at all.

And, as expected, the answer came. "No, thank 'e kindly, Nellie. It's awfully blowy, and awfully ... awfully *wide* open up there in them hills. Here, in this kitchen will do well enough for me."

This came as something of a revelation to Nellie. Apart from being the longest sentence from Sally that she'd heard in a long while, it struck her that perhaps her sister was afraid of open spaces.

Her heart opened in sympathy. This might explain a lot, and, as in the case of her seemingly being able to forecast the future, Nellie wondered if perhaps the treatment Sal had received at the hospital three years ago might have something to do with it.

She decided that this was something that might be better discussed with Penny.

Hugging her sister goodbye, and with a quick "Tell our mam where we've gone," she threw on her shawl and left.

She was gone before she could see her sister, placing her head on her arms at the table, a look of utter despair on her face.

They had left the town behind, and were now approaching the hills and wooded areas that Nellie loved. Soon, the two friends were the only passengers left on the tram as it rumbled to a stop.

On the way up, they had noticed how the pair of rather elderly horses had had to heave and strain between the shafts, as they reluctantly tackled the increasing hilliness of the terrain.

Troubled by this, Penny had asked the driver why he was still using the poor old things. "They ought to be out to pasture by now, surely," she'd said, with Nellie nodding in vigorous agreement.

"Eee, lassies," the man had replied. "Where've you been lately? Haven't y'heard? We're short of horses these days. The war has taken them all!"

The friends, making sympathetic but non-committal noises, exchanged glances. Experience had taught them that once one started telling people that they'd been at the Front, the eager questioning never ceased.

Taking note of their concern, and seeking to reassure them, the driver added, "We'll be getting mechanised soon enough, just like they're doing in the cities. Then all these poor old Dobbins will be out to grass, no doubt."

First watching to make sure that the pair had safely descended to the pathway, he politely touched the brim of his cap, before clicking at the horses to return homeward.

The girls smiled, as the horses, now finding themselves facing the downward journey, flickered their ears with pleasure before setting off.

Penny, watching them go, sighed. Nellie, with the intuition born of long friendship said quietly, "Gareth?"

"Aye, it's all this talk of horses. I'll always think of our Gary whenever I see a horse." Then she burst out in frustration, "I often wonder if I'll ever see him again. My poor brother!"

Gently, Nellie hooked her arm through that of her friend. "Come," she said, "we'll think of all our worries later. For now, let's seize this lovely day and enjoy it–just as though we had no worries at all."

Penny smiled, then taking in a deep breath, said, "Oh, the air is wonderful. No smog, no smoke, no guns, no noise–and just *look* at them trees!"

So entranced was she that she entirely forgot to correct herself. Nellie, noticing, chuckled softly. Then, arm in arm, the pair began their climb, upwards to the trees, now all ablaze in their autumn glory.

*   *   *

Tired from their walking, but still feeling the exhilaration imparted from the climb, the air, and the glorious autumn colours, the girls walked arm in arm down Nanton Street.

They were halfway down, and just approaching number 85, when Sally's head popped out of the door. She was looking up and down the street and, seeing them, began waving frantically before turning back into the house, leaving the door ajar.

Glancing at one another in sudden concern, the two girls increased their pace and were soon at the door.

Closing it behind them, they found themselves having to blink for a moment in the comparative darkness, after coming in from the bright sunlight.

Mam was at the table. Her head was bowed, and she was clutching at a letter, now crumpled in her hand. "Mam?" Nellie swooped towards the slumped form of her mother.

"Mam?"

"We've had a letter," Sally said. "I went to the mill and fetched Mam home. They let her go, considering ... considering ..." She faltered to a halt as Mam, emerging as if from a trance, straightened her back and looked up.

Very calmly, she said, "It's George," before her face crumpled into passionate tears.

Immediately, the three younger women converged upon her, patting and clucking their soothing sounds. Mam, however, was now sobbing uncontrollably and would not be comforted.

"Where is Pa?" Nellie asked.

"I asked, but they said he was out on an errand" Sally told her. "They'll let him know as soon as he gets back.

"Perhaps," she continued hopefully, "He'll be here soon."

Mam's crying fit seemed to be subsiding now, and one hand groped the air, while with the other, she lifted the corner of her apron, dabbing with it at her cheeks.

Instinctively, Penny grabbed for a tea towel, folded neatly at the sink. Handing it to Mam, she said softly, "Would you like me to go t'mill, and see if they will let my mam come?"

Accepting the towel gratefully, Mam buried her face in it, dabbing her tear-stained cheeks and blowing her nose ferociously.

Despite her anxiety, Nellie could not help but smile. She began to cough, in order to hide it. Mam would *never*, under normal circumstances, do such a thing as blow her nose on a tea towel ...

But then, she sobered, as the tears began to prick at her own eyes. She flicked them away with her fingers.

"No, no lovie." Mam reached up to Penny. "I'll not be troubling poor Alice. She has enough on her plate as it is." She managed a watery smile, giving Penny's hand a grateful little pat. "Pa'll be here soon enough, I'm sure."

Scarcely were the words out of her mouth, than Pa himself came flying through the door. He was winded and had obviously been running.

Gasping for air, and rubbing the stitch in his side, he crossed to Mam, who had risen from the table to greet him.

Silently, they embraced.

After a moment, Pa began to softly murmur, "Oh Jess, my lovie. Oh my dearest love."

Watching this intimacy between the couple, the three young women were stunned into silence.

Why, Nellie thought, *I can see how it must have been for them when they were young lovers.* She had never before seen this kind of intimacy displayed between her parents. They had always been discreet, and, to both her, and to her siblings, had never been "Jessie," or "Bill," but merely "Ma" and "Pa."

Now she could envisage what they must have once felt for one another–indeed, what they *still* felt for one another as together, they mourned the suffering of a child they had made.

Her heart jolted suddenly, as a vision of Harry came to her, alone, confused and wandering. She would be back at the Front soon, and *must* find him. She just *must.*

Looking about her now, she could see that Penny and Sally were touched by the sight before them and feeling awkward. This was a private moment, and not meant for them.

The three of them exchanged glances, then looking away, they moved quietly to the other side of the room.

"Shall us put on the kettle for tea?" It was the merest whisper from Sally.

Nellie shook her head–an unspoken "*No.*"

"Let's go up to our room, Sal," she said, indicating with a nod of her head for Penny to come, too.

There, all three of them sat on the beds–Sally on her own, the other two on Nellie's.

Her voice quivering, Nellie asked, "Does the letter say if he is dead, or wounded? And if wounded how ... how serious is it?"

"No, not dead, but wounded, but they don't give us any details–nothing at all!" Sally sounded frustrated. Penny and Nell glanced at one another, an unspoken sigh of relief passing between them. Things just *might* not be so bad after all.

Suddenly, Sally jumped up from her bed. "Oh my. I forgot–*you've* got a letter, too, our Nell. I don't know who it's from, but it's definitely not official, not like Mam's from the War Office."

She dived at the chest and, from the top drawer, hastily extracted a plain envelope.

Nellie seized it eagerly. "Why," Penny exclaimed, "that looks like Cilla's writing."

And, indeed it was.

Dear Nellie,

I do hope that both you and Penny are enjoying your break from all of this awfulness. I am off soon on a leave of my own, and might well be away before you are back. So, I thought I would send you this news before your parents receive the official notification from the War Office–they are not always forthcoming with the details!

Your brother George is here. He has been wounded, but these wounds are not too bad. No problems with either internal organs, or lost limbs. He has taken a bullet in his foot, and another in his shoulder. Both bullets have now been removed, and the wounds dressed. Indeed, Nurse Haines, knowing of our connections, has put me in charge of him. Just while I'm on duty, of course.

We have been able to talk quite a bit, and I know he is very proud of you. His main problem for now is the shell shock. You will be able to explain this to your parents– familiar as we all are by now with this unpleasant condition. Like our other patients, it seems to come and go. George can be perfectly rational (and, I must say, I find him charming) for a considerable amount of time, but when the guns are sounding in the distance, his panic can become quite uncontrollable, and it sometimes takes two orderlies to hold him while the panic lasts.

The good part of this, of course (and we must always look for the good), is that this means he will be going home. At first, to a convalescent home (I believe you mentioned a "Pembridge House" near your home?) and then, when the shell shock subsides, he will be able to return to your family. With any luck at all, the war should be over, one way or the other, within the year. I am praying that this will come to pass.

We are well enough over here–all things considered. Nurse Haines sends her kind regards to you both, and to your respective parents. I know that she regards the pair of you as being stalwart helpers, and is looking forward to your return.

Alas, there is no more news yet of either Gareth or Harry, but our wonderful stretcher-bearers are continuing to enquire constantly down the lines. Knowing Harry as we do, I can't help feeling that he must be continuing the good work of bearing the wounded somewhere down the lines. The while, I am certain, "chewing the cud" as it were, mulling over his, and your, situation.

I know that he loves you–as you love him–and that at the end of this period of tussling with himself, he might well return, perhaps when the war has ended, and seek you out. We can only hope that this will be so ... I shall continue to pray.

As for Gareth, there is so much talk of prisoners taken that have any experience with farming, or with animals generally, being seconded to work on farms in the German countryside. I have recently been given more stints of duty in the German ward now. Our bearers have been picking up so many of the German wounded, as they have been picking up ours (Isn't it all so stupid?). These are telling me that they have been hearing from home that (regarding the use of prisoners as farm workers) this is regularly being done.

With so many of their own lads taken for the war effort, any skilled worker is welcomed, "enemy" or no! Let us hope then, that this has been Gareth's fate–I shall continue to pray for him also.

Ah, the guns are rumbling again. Soon, the bearers will come with their sorry loads, so I'll stop now.

God bless you all.

Cilla.

*　　*　　*　　*

"Well, Alice, lovie–ain't that hopeful news!" Mam said, upon reading the letter from Cilla aloud for the umpteenth time–this time, for the benefit of Alice.

The family was seated around the kitchen table–Mam, Pa, Sally and Nell, as well as Alice and Penny, by now regarded as a natural extension of the Parkin household. Izzie, too, but today she was at work.

Twenty minutes earlier, Alice had come bustling in from the mill, her face full of concerned sympathy, ready to pick up the pieces of an emotionally devastated family. To her surprised pleasure, she had found them to be much more relaxed and happy than she had expected them to be, due to the arrival of Cilla's letter.

At the reading of Cilla's comments regarding Gareth, and the possibility of his working on a farm in Germany, Alice had gulped. Her hands had flown to her mouth, and the expression on her face had spoken clearly of her inner conflict. On the one hand, was the horror at him having been taken prisoner, and on the other hand, there was hope that he was not dead, or in a dreaded camp.

Finally, there was the dawning realisation, that even if he were a prisoner, then, as a valued farm worker, he would probably be treated well enough.

With that last thought, there came the dawning of actual hope. Her hands dropped to her lap, and she smiled–albeit somewhat weakly–at the assembled company.

"Eee, lass." Mam patted Alice's hand in approval. "That's the ticket then. While there's life, there's hope. Now," she continued, "all we have to worry about is our Will and"–with a sympathetic nod to Nellie–"Harry."

Pa and Alice nodded at this, as Mam went on. "As for our George, he'll be tickety-boo once he gets home again. We'll see to that, won't we, Pa?"

Once again, there were nods of approval all round, except for Nellie, who, biting her lip, refrained from saying what she really thought.

There was a slight, sympathetic glance from Penny. Both girls had, too many times, witnessed the plight of those men afflicted with shell shock. Both knew that there would be no hope of a quick cure. It would be a hard, long fight to get George back to anything resembling his former self.

Nellie could only cross her fingers, hidden in her lap, and hope for the best.

Now, though, she smiled to herself. She had noticed, with some amusement, Mam's reaction to Cilla's comment that she had found George to be "charming"–and to her mention of Harry.

Mam had had a gleam in her eye–the assessing look of a prospective mother-in-law, not to mention a grandmother. She had also exchanged quick glances with Pa, and Nellie was both amused and touched at seeing this gleam mirrored in Pa.

My, those two were so close these days, she thought. How had she not noticed this before? And then the certain knowledge came to her; they had been living for three years with the understanding that at least one of their offspring, if not all, might be lost to them.

A lump rose in her throat at the thought of the sheer, brave endurance of these parents–not only hers, but all over Britain, Germany, France, Belgium, Russia and, God bless them, Canada too.

Now, of course, there were also the Americans. Late arrivals though they were, with their stalwart help, this war *must* soon come to an end.

"You alright then, lovie?" Mam's voice broke into Nellie's reverie, and she startled back to attention. Several pairs of eyes were fixed enquiringly upon her–not the least of them Sally's.

Clearing her throat and attempting a smile, she waved a dismissive hand. "Oh, just daydreaming, Mam. It's been an exciting day, one way and another. I think, if you don't mind"–her glance swept round the assembled company–"I'll go up to bed now."

There was a general murmur of sympathetic assent, and Nellie stood, making an attempt at a casual-seeming stretch and yawn that soon turned into a genuine, full-bodied one. She realised only then, exactly how tired she really was.

Goodnights were said all round, and Alice, in the process of leaving, came across to where Nellie was standing at the foot of the stairs, preparing to ascend.

Gently, she touched Nellie's arm, giving it a squeeze. "Take care of yourself, dear Nell. You and Penny are having as rough a time of it as the men–people tend to forget that. Get some rest while you can, before ... before you have to leave us again."

Nellie knew instinctively that her friend and mentor was already grieving at the thought of having to say goodbye to her own daughter.

Taking Alice in her arms, she hugged her fiercely. "Oh Alice, *dear* Alice! Penny and I will look out for one another–I promise."

Nodding, biting her lip, Alice made for the door, reaching out for Penny to come home with her. Nellie watched them leave, then turned, ready to climb the narrow, steep staircase to the little room she shared, had always shared, with Sally.

She had not noticed the comprehending look that passed between her parents. They too, were preparing for the time, a mere ten days from now, when they would have to face their own goodbyes.

CHAPTER SIXTEEN
A Plot Is Hatched

Sally, already in her nightgown, was tucking herself into her bed beside the window. "G'night, our Nell," she said in a small voice.

Nellie paused in her ablutions for a moment. Was that a hint of tears? She was, however, far too tired to have to deal with any more dramas today. "G'night, our Sal," she murmured, and lifted the water jug, filling the earthenware basin on the washstand. Whatever might be troubling Sal, it would have to wait until morning, she thought. And this ungenerous response told her just how very tired she was.

Climbing into bed, she was fast asleep, even before her head hit the pillow.

Sometime later, she woke with a start. The church clock had just finished chiming its climb up to the hour, in a series of strokes. Now, there was a pause, then ... *ONE.*

One of the clock in the morning, her brain told her. But why did this wake her? Sally and she had lived with these chimes since they were babes in arms. So accustomed were they, indeed, that they rarely even registered them anymore.

Then, she heard it: a muffled, but persistent sobbing from the direction of Sally's bed. No sooner did she register this, than the sobs turned into a prolonged, though still muffled, wail.

Now thoroughly awake, Nellie struggled to sit, then swung her legs over the edge of her bed. "Sal–Sally ... What is it, sweetheart?"

Sally, hearing the concern in her sister's voice, now sat with her legs dangling over the edge of the bed. "Nell, oh *Nell*, I can't stand it anymore!"

Now thoroughly alarmed, Nellie reached out her arms to her sister. Sally then flung herself onto her knees, and into her sister's outstretched arms.

For perhaps a minute or two longer, Sally just cried and cried–muffling the sounds as best she could by crunching up the skirt of her gown and stuffing it into her face; this, so as not to wake her parents.

Nellie, saying nothing in particular, even though her anxiety had risen–as had her curiosity–merely rocked her weeping sister in her arms. She murmured every now and again, "Aye Sal, my poor lovie. Aye, Sal ..."

Gradually, the first fury of tears began to subside, to be replaced with hiccupping gulps.

Nellie pulled a handkerchief from under her pillow. "Here, Sal," she said.

Gratefully, Sally took this, and began to mop her reddened, tear-stained face.

Giving her a moment in which to recover herself, Nellie asked, "What is it, Sal? What's the problem?"

Taking a deep breath and squaring her shoulders, Sally looked her sister in the eye. "I can't stand it, Nell," she said. "I just can't *stand* it." Now the tears began again, but furiously, she swiped them away.

Nellie decided to give her time. She waited for a few moments, then asked, "Is it Robert? I hear he is married now, to that Marchmont woman."

Sally, startled, exclaimed, "Oh God, no–Vivienne Marchmont is welcome to him." Then, with a flash of humour, she added, "He is not so handsome now as he was before."

"I'm glad to hear you think so." Nellie had now connected Vivienne's name to that of the Lady in Blue, from that dreadful day just over three years before, and thought to herself: *Well, that avowal sounds healthy enough, anyway.*

"No," Sally, biting her lip, continued. "No, it's nothing to do with any of that. It's just … just … Oh *Nellie*, I can't stand it!"

Seeing Nellie's puzzled frown, she went on. "I just can't *stand* this place anymore. I want to get away!"

Nellie, alarmed, exclaimed, "Get away from what? Get away to where?"

"Oh, not Mam and Pa. Of course not them, but …" She heaved another sigh, trying to summon up the words she needed to explain her dilemma.

"It's this *place*, Eldenfield, the mill, the … the *narrowness* of it all." Her voice had risen, as her passion had increased, and Nellie put a warning finger to her lips.

Taking the hint that Mam and Pa might be disturbed, Sally quietened herself, before continuing. "I want *more–I* want to *do* more, *be* more! I don't want to stay here as some delicate flower that needs to be coddled and kept."

"But," Nellie interrupted, "darling Sal, you *earn* your keep here–you are such a help to Mam, with your scrubbing and cleaning and ironing …"

She was interrupted in turn by her sister, who whispered fiercely, "That's just *it*, our Nell. I keep thinking there must be more to life than this. I feel as though I'm hemmed in here, in this small world. You, Will and … and even our George–you've all got lives in the bigger world out there, but I am stuck, stuck, *stuck* here.

"Everyone is worrying about what's going on out there, but we can't *do* anything about it. Even Mam, and Pa and Alice are stuck. Izzie is stuck, working at that Brombridges store, all day, six days a week, serving all of them nobs with money to spend. And for *what*?"

Her voice had risen again, and again, Nellie put her finger to her own lips in warning.

With a frustrated shrug of her shoulders, Sally lowered her voice, but continued in what had, by now, become a tirade. Nellie understood this. She reached out and clasped one of her sister's hands–hands that had been moving restlessly in her lap, in concert with her rising anger.

"I'll tell you for *what,*" she continued, in her lower voice. "For the owners. For the likes of Robert Hoyle and his father, for the likes of *Lady* Charlotte Hoyle, and for Robert's toffee-nosed wife, bloomin' *Lady* Vivienne–that's *who!*

"T'aint for *us*–oh no, *we* are just pawns, the cogs in the wheel that keep things moving along at t'mill, that keeps bringing in the money that lets 'em all live in their bloomin' Pembridge House"–this, she said with a sneer–"so's they can swan around and grand it over us all!"

At last, she subsided, with a great, heaving sigh of unconsummated frustration. For a moment, there was total silence in the room.

Nellie regarded her sister with shining eyes. She was at once appalled, amazed, impressed and delighted at this sister that she has never seen before. A sister that hated school and learning of any kind, but who now was giving voice to exactly the sentiments she herself espoused. Sentiments shared until now with only Penny and Harry.

Unknown to both sisters at this time, they were sentiments that were stirring within the hearts of an increasing number of their fellow citizens...

"Oh *Sal,* my Sal!" Taking both of the hands, previously restless, but now lying clenched in Sally's lap, Nellie whispered, "I'm so *proud* of you."

Startled, Sally looked up. "Eh?" She searched Nellie's face for any traces of ironic dismissal. But there were none.

"Oh *Sal. You've* woken up. *Really* woken up. At last."

"Woken up?" Sally was bemused.

"Yes, my Sal. You've been through so much. You've *grown* so much. I ..."

"What are you saying? I'm the same. This place is the same. Nothing here changes ..." Abruptly, she pulled her hands from Nellie's grasp and sat, looking down at them, clenched once more in her lap, her body rigid.

Puzzled, Nellie frowned. There was another part of the mystery here, but she decided to leave well alone for the moment. Tomorrow would be another day.

The church clock sounded the chimes for two of the clock. Good heavens, tomorrow was already here. She yawned, briefly patting her sister's hands before rolling herself back into bed. "Try and sleep, Sal. Maybe we can talk again tomorrow?"

Without comment, Sally turned to sleep, pulling the bedclothes tightly around her neck, and burying her face once more into her pillow.

Soon, there was the sound in the room of gently buzzing snores.

*   *   *

"And she didn't seem to understand what you were trying to tell her?" Penny shook her head in puzzlement.

"No, she seems to be unable to perceive for herself just how much she has changed, how much she has grown in her thinking. I don't understand it, I just ... don't."

The friends were walking down the path that ran beside the canal. It was a rather dull day; the afternoon cast the light of a watery sun on the rows of barges, all waiting for the bundles of cloth from the mill. These would be loaded on the morrow.

The pair walked on in silence for a while, both of them lost in thought–each of them pondering the problem posed by Sally's frustrations.

Nell had confided to Penny her discussions with Sally on the previous night. Now, the pair was struggling to devise some kind of a plan of action–something that might, perhaps, help to alleviate Sally's distress. So far, nothing concrete had come to mind.

As they continued to make their way along the towpath, the gulls swooped around them, floating gracefully above the water. Every now and then, someone would notice something edible lying on the pathway–a crust, a tiny scrap of meat–and would swoop down to inspect it, before seizing it in his beak.

Immediately, there would come the sound of squawking from another member of the flock. Down he would swoop, and then the squabbling would commence. This raucous confrontation would, in turn, attract more birds ...

Wheeling and shrieking–ignoring the mere humans standing by and smiling, as they watched this cacophonous show–they would continue until, with a final, triumphant gulp, the morsel would be consumed. Then, the whole gang would soar skywards once more, an aerial ballet in perpetual motion.

"This is a sign of bad weather at sea." Penny, still smiling, imparted this scrap of information.

"Really?" Nellie stood, hands in pockets, peering into the sky.

"Yes." Penny nodded wisely. "It's supposed to be a portent of colder weather coming".

"Brrr ... I think they are right!" Nellie's hands dug further into her pockets. "Let's go home–I could do with a nice hot cup of tea".

Linking arms, still talking, trying to puzzle out some solution to Sally's problems, the pair turned homewards.

The gulls, still squawking, continued to wheel and turn in a darkening sky.

*   *   *

"Mam, can I speak to you for a moment? While Sally's not here?"

Nellie and her mother were sitting at the kitchen table, sharing a last cup of tea before Mam bustled off to work. Sally was outside in the tiny back yard. She was wringing the wet wash through the mangle, hoping to peg them out in the breeze.

Surprised, Mam looked up from her sipping. "Why, lass–looks like you've got a secret on your mind." She laughed, preparing to hear the joke.

Nellie shook her head. "No, Mam. There's something wrong–it's not a joke. It's about Sally and ... and I think it might be serious."

Instantly, the genial expression faded from Mam's face. Now, both women turned towards the yard door, but it remained closed. Mam leaned earnestly toward her daughter.

"Tell me then, child. What have you noticed?"

Taking a deep breath, Nellie launched into a reprisal of her midnight conversation with her sister, carefully editing out some of the angrier remarks, the kind that might be hurtful to Mam and Pa.

When she had finished, Mam, far from being surprised, nodded her head thoughtfully. "Pa and me was beginning to worry a bit. She does seem to have been not quite her usual self lately–I mean, the kind of self she'd become just before you left."

She lowered her voice, glancing briefly again at the back door. Then she turned to Nellie and said, "Pa and me was wondering if it might not be that ... that Robert." Her voice expressed scorn. "Him what did for her in the first place. We was wondering if it were because he were back, and were wounded, like ..."

She stopped as Nellie shook her head. "No, Mam, I asked her that, but she was most insistent that it was not him that she is worried about."

Nellie frowned, thinking. "She just doesn't seem to want to speak about what might be wrong." She paused for a moment, trying to express herself clearly. "But I do feel strongly that Sal wants a change in her life."

"Mmm." Mam was nodding. "Aye, lass, I've felt that, too. But"–she frowned–"what could she do? Where could she go? She doesn't have a good education, not like you. All she has is her looks–and that's more likely to get her into trouble than help her get on in the world."

She leaned back in her chair, sniffing her motherly disapproval at a world that would be likely to take advantage of her lovely daughter.

"Well now, Mam." Nellie leaned forward, an earnest expression on her face. "I've been thinking hard about that. Something has happened to our Sal that is quite remarkable." Mam leaned forward in interest as Nellie, struggling to express herself, began to explain.

I believe that it might, just *might,* have something to do with that treatment of hers three years ago." As Mam raised her eyebrows in doubt, she hastened on. "No, Mam, hear me out.

"You know, of course, that I've been working with many of the men at the Front who are suffering in the same way as our George ..."

She paused in sympathy for a moment, as her mother winced at the thought, then continued. "Well, I've been doing a lot of reading–reading about the brain–and there is some discussion going on about the effects of these shocks. They can cause amnesia, but in some cases they can open up connections in the brain that can really help a person think more clearly ..."

"Eee, lass!" Mam was now thoroughly engaged, her eyes shining. "And you think that's what's happening to our Sal?"

"Well, it *might* be." Nellie didn't want to stir up any false hopes. "There's an awful lot of argumentation going on at the moment. People are either for, or very much against exploring that kind of thinking."

Mam's face fell and she quickly added, "Oh, but I just have a feeling that we are on the verge of exploring the brain in ways never thought of before!" She sighed in frustration. "I just wish I had more education. I want to know so much more ..." She smiled wryly to herself, thinking how like that statement was to the ones Sally had been making last night.

She was about to explain to her mother that another side effect of these treatments was that they tended to induce feelings of anxiety. Something that Sally had definitely demonstrated to her with her angry reclusiveness.

They were interrupted, however, by a *click* as the latch on the back door was lifted. Rushing to finish her thoughts, Nellie continued, "Penny and I were wondering if she could not, perhaps, work up at Pembridge House. I think she could manage the work–" She broke off in mid-sentence, as Sally, flushed from working outside, entered the warm kitchen.

Peering at Nellie over a huge pile of wet laundry, she started to say, "It'll not be a good drying day today, our Nell, we'll have to use the–Oh!" Surprised at seeing her mother, she said, "Mam, y'ere going to be late."

She dumped half of her bundle into the waiting arms of her sister, who had scrambled to her feet to help.

"Aye, Sal, lass!"

Mam heaved herself to her feet, pushing on the tabletop to help herself rise.

Nellie bit her lip. Seeing how tired and old her mother seemed now, she felt her own anger rising inside her.

A quick glance at Sally confirmed that she was feeling the same.

"Well"–Mam was at the door–"I'll see you two lasses t'night, then."

A shadow of her old twinkle crossed her face, and then she was gone, clicking the latch behind her.

Exchanging glances once more, the sisters heaved down the rack stored in the ceiling. This, for use on those days when the weather would not be co-operating in the drying process.

Expertly, from long-accustomed habit, the pair draped the items for drying in proper order–female undergarments hidden behind the larger sheets and towels, out of view from any neighbouring male who might visit on this day.

They worked quickly and in silence, finally hauling at both ends in unison, until the items were hanging neatly from the rack. Then hauling once more, they tucked the rack back up into the ceiling area.

Work accomplished, they heaved a sigh and, rubbing at their aching arms, sat down opposite one another at the table.

For a moment, silence was maintained. Then, "You see–you see what I mean?" Sally was beside herself once more, biting her lip, shaking her head and clenching her fists in anger.

"I do–oh, I *do.*" Nellie reached across the table, clasping her sister's hands, cold still from the outside work. "I'll make us a cuppa and we'll talk, Sal."

Sally shook her head. She was drooping in misery. "There's now't you can do for me our Nell." Then she burst forth, "I'm just useless, useless, *useless!*"

Her fists were now pounding the table in a fury of frustrated self-blame.

Getting up from her chair, Nellie moved around the table. Placing herself behind her sister and taking hold of her shoulders, she began to knead them–softly at first, but with increasing strength–a technique imparted from watching Cilla at work.

As she worked, she hummed–a wordless, repetitive crooning also picked up from Cilla.

Slowly, Sally's body began to soften–a classic indication of someone beginning to relax. Finally, she heaved an enormous, life-renewing sigh, filling her lungs with oxygen.

"Thank you, Nellie." She smiled up at her sister. "Thank you."

Returning the smile, Nellie gave a final grip to the shoulders, shaking them a little and then patting them before releasing her hold.

"Now, our Sal, I'm putting on the kettle and we're *going* to talk!"

* * *

"It was amazing." Nell and Penny were once more beside the canal. Dirty as the water was–the effluent of industry being very much in evidence–there was a bustling, warm-hearted atmosphere here.

The bargemen were busy, receiving their loads from the warehouse men, and there was much good-natured joshing going on between them.

"Eee, wilt thou mind yer back there, Sam. That's t'second time ye've nearly dropped t'load in t'canal! Wait there, now, while I get our Bessie out t'way."

To the aforementioned Bessie, he said, "Gid up there, old gal. Mind yer big feet now on t'ropes. Here we go now. Stay thee there, gal, 'til we get this load aboard."

The endlessly patient old plod horse would snort through her nose, gratefully accepting the offered lump of sugar or piece of apple from her bargeman.

Then, there would be the usual new apprentice, clumsily bewildered at the teasing of the older men and blushing furiously until they would relent.

"Never thee mind, lad–we've all been there in our time. Stand thee there, lad, by our old Bessie and our Ned. Keep 'em company, lad, until it's time for us to go."

Then, winking at the other men, he added, "Y'can watch the *experts,* lad. See how things are done!"

Then, the men would all guffaw, clapping the boy on his shoulders as they passed by. The horses would snort at the sounds of merriment, nodding their heads as if in cahoots with the men.

Even the two young women, watching from a discreet distance all of this busy hullabaloo, were smiling.

At last, all was done. Large rolls of woolen fabric–the result of their mothers' labours–were safely stowed aboard. Horses, standing in patient line were hitched.

The cry went up, "Giddy hup, hup, *hup* now," and the barges creaked slowly into motion–horses, heads down, massive shoulders straining, as farewells were shouted between the bargemen and their warehouse workmates.

Now, as the eternally ravenous seagulls came shrieking down, seeking the detritus left from the workers lunch, the girls turned homeward.

"So, we have a plan, and Sally agreed?" Penny was matching her pace to Nellie's. Both of them were anxious to get home.

Nellie had already imparted to Penny her conversation of the morning. "Well, if she manages to keep up her courage, yes, we have a plan. Oh, I hope we can help her. She *can't* go on being as depressed and reclusive as she's been 'til now."

Nellie smiled at the concerned response from her friend. "You're a good soul, Penny. I thank you."

"Oh, it's nothing, Nell. After all we've been through together, we're joined at the hip by now."

Laughing, the pair linked arms while they journeyed. As they walked, Nellie went over their plans.

"So tomorrow, after Mam and Pa have left, we are going up the hill to Pembridge House, all three of us. T'was the thought of George being there that finally convinced our Sal."

"Aye, Nellie. Let's just hope she's still of the same mind when we get back!"

CHAPTER SEVENTEEN
To Pembridge House

"Darling, you mustn't stay out too long. It *is* October, after all."

Solicitously, Vivienne leaned over her husband, as he lay back in the lawn chair set up for him.

"Oh damn it, Viv. Don't cluck at me. Sometimes you're worse than a barnyard full of bloody hens."

Vivienne bit back a retort of her own. She had learned from experience, not to cross this wealthy "catch" of a man. Papa was depending on this marriage. It would be a way of helping the aristocratic house of Marchmont out of their ever-present fiscal difficulties.

It had been impressed upon her, from an early age, that it would be her duty to "marry well." Her mother, aunts and various other "gentlewomen" of their acquaintance–most of them in equally straitened circumstances–had made it their business to never let her forget.

She remembered vividly the day when, at the age of fifteen and already a budding beauty, her father had looked at her with new eyes–eyes that had held a speculative gleam.

He had never before shown any real interest in her. She knew that he had never forgiven her for not being a boy. Nor yet, had he ever forgiven his wife for being unable to produce the son and heir he had so longed for.

Once she had turned seventeen, however, and noticing how this daughter of his had blossomed at last into her full beauty, his desperately calculating mind had seen her as a commodity. Someone–or rather, some*thing*–that he could use in his pursuit of accruing enough wealth to shore up his sagging fortunes.

And so, at the tender age of seventeen, Vivienne had joined the ranks of the "Debutante Dance." Parties were attended; parties were given. Young bachelors, scions of their houses, were encouraged by their families, to seek a "suitable" bride.

This, in turn, would lead to the bearing of sons and daughters who, especially the sons, would carry on the bloodlines, that for centuries, had sustained the ruling classes.

The times were changing, though. So many of the landed gentry were now losing, for various reasons, their positions of privilege. This sense of privilege had been held for so long as a matter of course, that at first they had had difficulty in comprehending the fact that they were, indeed, under threat.

Now, however, the realisation had dawned that new strategies must be employed, if the great houses of England were to survive.

Educated young men–not necessarily of ancient lineage, but with wealth in their background–were no longer to be spurned as "upstarts." Indeed, they were increasingly being sought after as possible suitors for the daughters of the aristocracy.

Families such as the Marchmonts.

That the Hoyle wealth had been obtained by "mere" trade was tactfully ignored. After all, if a young woman of aristocratic lineage, but poor, were to marry a young man of like lineage, but also poor, what would be the sense of that?

The unfortunate couple, sans wealth, would merely be reduced to the ranks of the middle classes–something that must *not* be countenanced.

And so, late in the August of 1914, Vivienne and Robert, invited to the same party, had met.

This meeting was duly noted by their observant elders. Sir Richard, and the Earl of Marchmont had met. Discussions ensued. Lawyers were called in, papers drawn up and voila! A marriage had been brokered.

Robert, though not exactly overjoyed, was well enough pleased. He understood his father's hopes that by this marriage, the Hoyle family might rise in the world's estimation. Surely, too, the woman was lovely enough–she reminded him, indeed, of someone who ... oh, what was her name? Never mind ...

Vivienne had been pronounced by the doctors as being still a virgin, and as being healthy enough that she could bear him sons. Yes, she would do well enough. He would look forward to their wedding night.

As for Vivienne, if she had any qualms, she kept them to herself. The fact that Mama and Papa were so overjoyed gave her pleasure, and she delighted in being, at last, an object of her father's approval.

The marriage had taken place during the course of Robert's first leave, early in 1915. As in so many of the weddings taking place in that time of war, it was a quiet affair, taking place in the chapel of Marchmont Castle.

Just a few members of the family attended, plus staff and some of the locals from the village.

The wedding night was a nightmare–at least for Vivienne. Like most girls of this time, she had only the very sketchiest notion of what would be taking place. When it came, it was violent and demanding, and over very quickly.

She was bloody and sore. He was as satisfied as he ever was with anything–that is to say, not so very satisfied and wanting more.

The initial deed accomplished, though, he had the grace to let her be for the moment, merely slapping her on the bottom, and turning on his side to sleep.

She lay beside him very much awake. He was snoring now, having drunk more than enough at the wedding feast.

Gradually, her body began to relax. So, this is it, she thought, and wondered how she was going to endure the years of "wedded bliss" ahead ...

There were no signs of an early pregnancy and, soon enough, Robert was back at the Front, returning only once he had been wounded.

Between his recovery time from the wound and now his bout of the flu, there had been precious little time for any concentrated lovemaking, and so, much to the concern of both families, she had remained a barren woman.

"Another blanket, my dear?" Tentatively, she held up a rug, hoping to place it over his shoulders. "It really is beginning to get colder now."

Vivienne was keeping patience with her father's approval. If she were to lose him–his "investment"–now, before she had borne him a grandson, she knew with certainty that all warmth, all approval, would be withdrawn at once, never to return.

"Blast you, woman! Why the hell can't you just leave me *alone!*" Throwing the blanket roughly on the ground, he limped back into the house.

Sighing, Vivienne bent and picked up the blanket.

She wouldn't cry. She would *not* show weakness of any sort. She knew from experience that this would only fuel his irrational exasperation, and that he would despise her for it.

The three young women, fresh from toiling up the long drive-way, were just in time to hear Robert's tetchy remark, and they exchanged meaningful glances.

From the corner of her eye, Vivienne, in the act of folding the blanket and turning into the house, noticed their presence. Laying the blanket on the chair, she hastened to meet them.

Robert, when in one of these moods, must not be disturbed. Forcing a hospitable smile, and noticing that Nellie, at least, was in her Red Cross uniform, she invited them into the house.

She had assumed that they were there on some Red Cross business, but Nellie, taking the lead, explained their mission.

Immediately, Vivienne led them into the library and ordered tea. "You must be exhausted, my dears, making such a journey on foot."

Nellie, remembering the many, many times she had made the same journey, early in the mornings and late at night, suppressed a smile. She knew that Penny must be doing the same.

"So." Vivienne was regarding Sally, groping for a reason as to why she somehow seemed familiar. "You are seeking a position at the house in order to be near your brother when he arrives from the Front?"

Dumbly, overcome by the proximity of this "Lady in Blue," a woman who exuded kindly–and yes, authoritative–interest, Sally nodded.

"My sister is a little shy, but she is an excellent worker," Nellie hastened to say.

"Yes, indeed, I too can attest to that. She runs the household while her mam and pa are at the mill." This from Penny.

Dressed in her civilian clothes, Penny had reverted to the stylish being she had been at Pembridges. A hat, perched cheekily atop her head, finished off an ensemble that would have done justice to the lady herself.

Now, Vivienne's attention was turned towards Penny, regarding her with interest. "And you, my dear, you are also seeking employment?"

"Oh, well, I ..."

Penny got no further, before Vivienne continued with enthusiasm. "I am currently seeking someone to take the position of lady's maid. Most unfortunately, the previous holder of that position has decided to return to her home in France. Despite the danger, she feels, understandably, that she should be with her family at this time.

"I quite understand, of course," she continued "but it has, I'm afraid, left me rather bereft." Here, she smiled, charmingly apologetic. "I had come to rely on her so much."

Nellie, without even looking at her friend, sensed the yearning in her at the thought of doing something so "up her street," as Mam would have put it.

Turning to Penny, she said, meaningfully, "I think you should take this, if it is an offer." And, before Penny, open-mouthed, could say anything at all, she continued, "You see, Lady Vivienne, we are both of us Red Cross nurses, and it is difficult to get out of our contracts. "*But*," she added with emphasis as Penny, gasping like a fish, and so obviously torn between duty and desire, tried to say something,

"I do believe that this is the kind of thing my friend was born to do. If you are serious"–with another meaningful look at Penny–"I'm certain that she would do an excellent job."

The tea had arrived, complete with buttered scones, jam and sponge cake. Such a tea as the three young women could only dream about in the usual course of their lives.

Over tea, and when Vivienne had finished laughing, they discussed the details of how things might proceed. "I'm sure that Lady Charlotte, my mother-in-law, you know"–the girls nodded–"will be able to manage the Red Cross very nicely. We could get you freed up and ready to start very soon, *if*"–here she looked closely at Penny–"you really want to come and be my maid."

Putting down her tea cup, and finishing swallowing her last crumb of sponge cake, Penny delicately wiped her mouth on her napkin. "Yes, Lady Vivienne," she said. Then "Oh, *yes*! Indeed, I would."

"Then so you shall." Laughing again, Vivienne turned her attention now towards Sally. "And you, my dear, would you be averse to working in the kitchens? We have great need now of good workers there with so many hungry men to feed, including, of course, your brother when he arrives."

Sally, still somewhat overwhelmed, but beginning to recover her composure, first nodded, and then, finding her voice, said clearly, "Yes, Lady Vivienne, I would like that very much."

For just a moment, the sound of Sally's voice seemed to touch something deep inside Vivienne. Automatically, and without thinking, one hand reached up to stroke her face where once there had been a scar.

Nellie's stomach clenched. *Oh God, dear God*, she prayed, *don't let her remember* ...

The moment passed, however, pleased as Vivienne was to have achieved an agreement with Penny. From the very first glance, her every instinct had told her that this was a person who would be a loyal and talented employee. And mostly, her instincts were never wrong.

Sally was quiet on the way home.

Penny, on the other hand, was bubbling between joy at being given this chance in life-no more Pembridges, and cream tea every day!-and guilty regret at leaving Nellie to travel alone, to face again the dangers of the Front without her.

Nellie reassured her as best she could, resolutely tamping down the small, ungenerous spurts of jealousy that would keep flaring up from time to time.

"Don't be silly, Penn. You deserve this chance. It's so ... *you*."

Penny threw her a grateful look then, drawing closer, linked arms with her and said, "You're a good friend, our Nellie. The *best*."

Warmed by this gladly given token of friendship, Nellie squeezed Penny's arm before turning to Sally, trudging wordlessly beside them.

"Hey, our Sal. Aren't you glad they took you on?"

Sally stopped dead in her tracks. "A kitchen maid." She sounded glum. "Just a little *kitchen* maid!"

Extricating herself from Penny's arm, Nellie turned to her sister. Then, taking her shoulders, she looked deep into Sally's eyes.

Sally avoided the intended eye contact by staring at the ground, still saying not a word.

"Now, our Sal," Nellie's words were gentle but firm. "'Tis a chance for you, too." When Sally raised her head sharply, ready to protest, she stopped her. "Yes, Sally, but a kitchen maid is only the beginning. If you play your cards right, you could easily move up the ranks. You've got it in you, you know. I've watched you at work at home" Here she gave her sister a little shake. "You are quick, quiet and efficient. Just what they like in these big houses."

"*Invisible*, you mean!"

Once again, Nellie wondered at her sister's bitterness. Where did it come from?

"Sally, lovie. You could move up to being a housekeeper, or a lady's maid like Penny. These are quite important positions, you know. You would be regarded as a professional."

Sally gave her sister a sad little smile. "Aye, our Nellie. If you say so."

She stopped in her tracks, biting her lip, then, reaching out to touch Nellie's hand, she added "Thank you, Nell, I'll believe you then." But there were tears in her eyes.

Penny had been watching this interchange with compassionate interest. But now, the sound of the approaching tram reached her ears.

"Oh, hurry, *hurry*–we'll have to wait for *ever* if we miss this one!"

Now, the three of them, picking up their skirts, ran down the rest of the hill like the wind.

CHAPTER EIGHTEEN
Soon Time to Go

"Well, that's just wonderful, my lovie."

Sitting on a couple of upturned boxes in the storeroom, Mam and Alice were taking a brief break from their labours.

The storeroom door had to be left open, of course, to satisfy the watching eyes of those who would be only too willing to report that the break, brief as it needed to be, had taken too long.

Even Alice, long-standing as she was, was subject to this indignity. Too long, and money would be docked from their pay–no excuses accepted.

Despite the fact that the open door allowed the constant clack and hum of industry to impinge upon their conversation, the two women were happily engaged in discussing this new turn of events, the good fortune that had fallen upon their children.

"Aye," Alice, replying to Mam's comment, continued, "I can hardly believe it myself. Oh, I'm *that* pleased for our Penn. It's the chance of a lifetime for her. She's up for the challenge–I know it. I've always known it!

"And then there's your Sal. She's a real good little worker that one. She'll be rising up from kitchen maid in no time at all, just you wait and see ..."

She stuttered to a stop, overcome by joyous emotion, and Mam reached out to her in sympathy, squeezing her hand. With all of the shared emotional ups and downs of the past few years, the women had become fast friends.

Pa, passing the open door, moved to shut it. Then, seeing the two women, he nodded, smiling his understanding.

Raising five fingers–an unspoken *"Five minutes more, ladies,"* he closed the door just a little further, allowing them more privacy. Then, he was gone.

Mam smiled. "He's a good man, is my Bill."

Alice, echoing the smile, agreed. "Aye, Jessie, lass, he is. One of the best." Then, "And Sally, how does she *really* feel about starting in the kitchen?"

Mam frowned worriedly. "Well, she doesn't exactly seem to be overjoyed. Me and our Nell were talking about it last night, and she told me that she'd had a good chat with Sal, explained to her like that she'd nowhere to go but up." She sighed. "It didn't seem to cheer her, though."

Alice frowned in thought, then said, "Dost thou think, Jess, that the poor wee scrap could be worrying that someone might remember her, for what happened at the beginning of t'war?"

"Aye, our Nellie were thinking that. But then, as she said, being tucked away in t'kitchen like, at least in the beginning, she'll be out of sight, out of mind."

"Aye, and be the time she's risen up a bit, so much water will have gone under the bridge that it won't hardly matter." Alice was being resolutely determined to look on the bright side. Nothing would be allowed to spoil the pleasure of these moments.

Pa opened wide the door. Shaking his head, and wearing a mock frown, he indicated that time was up by looking at the non-existent watch on his wrist, before moving on.

Sighing, creaking up from their unaccustomed sitting position, the pair returned to the clatter and rumble of their day-to-day work.

*　　*　　*

"Oh, my. There always seems to be a lot of turning about in this family these days, what with George coming home at last, and now you, our Nell, having to leave before he's even got here ..."

Mam, Pa and Nellie were seated around the kitchen table. The inevitable pot of tea was being passed around by Mam. She fluffed affectionately at Nellie's hair as she filled her cup.

"Aye." Pa was in agreement with Mam. "'Tis a great shame ye'll be missing our George at his homecoming. Just by a day or two it seems." Sighing, he shook his head.

Looking at him, Nellie could see clearly, that he badly needed rest. Catching Mam's eye, she could see that her mother thought so, too. Nellie decided to introduce a more cheerful note.

"Well, I'm so glad that Penny will be there to cheer him on. And there's our Sal, busy upstairs packing. She'll be there, too. He'll be glad of that."

She did not mention to her already emotionally burdened parents that George was going to need all the care the family could give him.

There would be time for them to understand that later ...

"How do y'think our Sal is feeling about going up to work at the Big House, our Nell?" Pa, his brow furrowed, looked enquiringly at his elder daughter. "After all, 'cept fer that stay over at t'hospital, she's never been away from home fer long at all."

Nellie considered for a moment, then said, "Well, I think she has a mixture of feelings for now. She's glad that she'll be earning *and* getting her keep."

She smiled briefly, thinking of all those cream teas in Sally's future.

"I think, though, that she is somewhat worried at what might happen if Lady Vivienne ever puts two and two together and remembers what she did that day at the parade."

She had not mentioned to her parents, the nasty scene between Robert and Vivienne that she, Penny and Sally had witnessed the other day. Nor did she feel she should tell them of her worries concerning Robert's state of mind.

Even more than any worries regarding Vivienne–who, it seemed to her, was a stable, fair-minded young woman–Nellie's worry was that Robert might lash out at a vulnerable Sally. Worse, that he might attempt, out of boredom, to seduce her once more.

None of these thoughts, she decided, should be shared for now with Mam and Pa. Crossing her fingers under the table, she hoped that time would take care of these things in the end.

There was the bump, bumping sound of a heavy suitcase being hauled down the stairs, and Sally's voice announcing, "I'm ready!"

Pa, rising from the table, hurried over to help his daughter manoeuvre her luggage down the last few steps. Puffing jokingly, he said, "*My*, lass–hast kitchen sink in there, then?"

Everyone, including Sally, laughed.

"Eee, lass." Mam, opening her arms wide, embraced her daughter, kissing her gently on the forehead. "I'll miss thee, my lovie. I'll miss thee ever so much, but ..." She sighed. "'Tis a good thing that you are doing for yourself. 'Twill give you a real good start in life. Better'n at mill, I can tell thee!"

"Aye, Mam, I know." Sally nodded, smiling, though somewhat tearfully. "But I'll be back every first Sunday in t'month, regular as clockwork, you'll see!"

"Aye, lass, and I'll make thee my best stew ever. Just for you." Hastily, she wiped a few tears away with the edge of her apron. "Now, off y'go, my pet, and I'll see thee in a month."

It had been arranged, as Penny had already started at Pembridge, that Pa and Nellie would accompany Sally on the tram journey. Then, at the beginning of the long driveway up to the house, they would say their goodbyes.

Most thoughtfully, Vivienne had arranged for a pony and cart to meet her. She would not, of course, be delivered to the house by the front door. The cart would drop her off at the servant's entry at the back.

Pa had had his arm firmly around his younger daughter's shoulders all the way in the tram. Nellie noticed that his hands were trembling as he now hauled out the case for delivery to the driver of the cart. Her heart went out to him.

With a click of his tongue, the driver of the tram, instructed his horses to turn, then stand, waiting to make their journey back.

The young lad on the cart, seeing the pretty girl he was to carry, jumped down eagerly. Seizing the heavy case from Pa, he lifted it high in the air, throwing it in the back as though it were as light as a feather.

He then made a respectful little bow, introducing himself as "I be Billy–I be the under gardener."

He then lifted the surprised Sally -also as lightly as if she had been a feather–up onto the seat beside him. Raising his whip in salute, he cracked it in the air, and the ancient pony, with a flick of his ears, began to lumber slowly up the hill.

Pa and Nellie waved, calling "Goodbye, goodbye! See you soon" and then the cart, carrying its precious burden, disappeared behind some trees.

There was a gulp from Pa, and Nellie took his hand, squeezing it and shaking it gently. He gulped again, and then smiled, squeezing back. The tram driver, having waited long enough, gave a gruff "All aboard," and they were on their way back to town.

At first, Mrs. Perkins had been somewhat affronted. It wasn't the place for the young Lady Vivienne to make such a decision. It was the place of Lady Charlotte to approach her housekeeper with the news that a new, young scullery maid had been hired.

Charlotte, however, had made her peace with the woman. Like her husband, Sir Richard, she understood how difficult their son could be. She had watched in sympathy, as it had become more and more apparent, that he was not treating his new bride as she deserved to be treated.

So, if her young daughter-in-law had taken it into her head to engage two, untried young women from the town into her employ, well, it *was* only two, and no harm done.

Tactfully, she had approached the bristling Bessie Perkins and, having a talent for it, had made her peace.

The housekeeper was as ready to be charmed by her mistress as were most people that came into her circle. Charlotte did, indeed, have a talent for peacekeeping. A talent that Robert most certainly did not share.

Sir Richard, now more than ever, with the huge extra burden of being in charge of so many ailing men and with the staff needed to cope with them, was most thankful for his wife's support.

So it was with Bessie Perkins. Recovering now from her former state of mind, she had decided that this was no time to be aggrieved at having to train up a new girl.

I'll give her a chance, she had thought to herself. *Perhaps she might even turn out to be useful.*

Now, at the sound of the cart approaching the back door, and hearing the crack of Billy's whip, she smoothed down her apron and, putting a smile on her face stood, ready to open the door, and welcome this newcomer in.

CHAPTER NINETEEN
Nellie Must Leave

Nellie had said her somewhat tearful goodbyes to Penny before she had left for Pembridge House. This, a day or two before Sally's departure.

Vivienne had obviously been in a great hurry to establish Penny as her lady's maid. An excited Penny had been equally desirous to begin.

Now, on a crisp, late October day, the time had come for Nellie to return to the Front.

Her mind was very much divided. On the one hand, and much to her surprise, she found herself almost looking forward to getting back–back to the valuable work of tending, comforting and supporting the men in her charge. Watching them begin to heal, or comforting them as they lay dying ...

Also, of course, there were the friends she had made: Cilla, Nurse Haines and several others, medics among them. With these, she had formed a bond, as together they had fought furiously to cope with the influx of incoming wounded–and the next influx, and the next, until one group of crying, gasping bodies, merged into another. In the end, their would-be healers, were themselves almost dying on their feet from exhaustion.

Yes, these men were her friends in battle, and she bonded with them, as the fighting men had bonded with *their* comrades in arms.

Then, of course, there was Harry ... Ah, but no–she quelled the sudden surge of hope that had momentarily filled her being with longing. She could not think of him yet. She would go back and get on with her own, personal war, until all was over and done with. Perhaps then, if they were both still alive ...

Perhaps ...

On the other hand, this was her home. Her friends and family here, in this place, called out to her heart, and she could weep at having to say goodbye yet again.

As well, the growing professionalism she had been gaining for the last three years badly wanted to see exactly what condition George was in. Was he even redeemable? So many of these poor victims of shell shock just never seemed to recover. So many of them seemed condemned to live a half-life, beset by fear, anxiety and unresolved anger.

Better to die than that, she found herself thinking, then pulled up short in shock. What had she just thought? How could she, a healer, wish death on George, or anyone else?

Trembling, she sat down on the bed, breathing deep, slow breaths–the calming technique taught to her by Cilla.

Slowly, methodically, she re-commenced tightening the straps on her suitcase. There was no use in wishing. George would be arriving tomorrow.

She, was leaving today.

CHAPTER TWENTY
Life at Pembridge House

"Now, child, when either of our two mistresses come–Lady Charlotte, or Lady Vivienne–not that they do come very often, ye bow yer head, and you curtsey, like this."

Bessie Perkins, comfortably stout and with floury hands, primly held out her skirt, doing a little bob.

"See?"

"Aye, thank you".

"Well, now *you* try."

Gathering her skirt, Sally did a deep curtsey–the sort she and Nellie used to do when, as children, they had played at being princesses.

"Nay, *nay*, lass!" The voice was sharp, but there was a twinkle in Bessie's eye. "Ye just do a little bob. Just like I showed you just now. Remember, y're a servant girl, not a grand lady."

Sally must have shown the smallest flicker of resentment, very briefly, before regaining control of her features.

Bessie smiled. Then she said, "Now, now, my lass. There's nowt wrong with being a good servant. Especially not now, when staff is so short-handed. Why, only the other day, Lady Charlotte confided in me that we servants–the good ones mind–are like gold dust these days.

"Besides," she continued, "'tis better'n working at t'mill! Now, wouldn't you agree?"

Meekly, Sally nodded. She liked this woman. Bessie had greeted her warmly, and made sure she felt comfortable and, yes, *wanted*.

She was beginning to understand why. Last night, Agnes, her roommate, had explained in detail the way things used to be in the hierarchy of the house.

Butler and housekeeper at the top of the pecking order, cook next, followed by footmen, lady's maid, parlour maids, pot-boys and kitchen maids inside. Head gardener, under gardener, gardener's boys and stable hands were outside.

"Eee, it were great–so many of us all working away for the family, and they so kind. You won't find a better master or mistress than Sir Richard and Lady Charlotte!"

Agnes's eyes had fairly sparkled with enthusiasm, and Sally's heart had warmed to her. She couldn't help thinking, however, how incredible it was, having so many people all serving a family of just two parents and one brat of a son.

She thought of the Hoyles, and of others of their ilk. And she found herself comparing these privileged lives with the lives of Mam and Pa, of Alice and the other working people that she knew. It didn't seem *fair*, and indeed, it wasn't fair.

Just for a moment, the old feelings of frustration and helpless anger rose up within her, but she pushed the thoughts down, merely saying "And now?"

Agnes was only too happy to oblige this prettily attractive novice to the ranks. "Well now, it's the war. Just spoiled *everything* it has. The men got took away for the fighting like, including my Frank. He ... he ..."

She faltered, and just for a moment, her cheerful manner left her. She gulped, and then went on. "He were killed in one of the first battles. My poor Frank."

In a flood of warm sympathy, Sally held out her arms towards her new friend.

Agnes only smiled, however. Shaking her head, she said, "Eee, thanks, lass, but it were three years gone now. I still miss him, of course, but ... well, life goes on, doesn't it?"

Before Sally could say more, Agnes continued–sounding, Sally thought with some amusement, rather like an elder sister. "Now, bedtime, lass. We'll be up in the morn come five o' clock, and on duty before six, so we must get our beauty sleep while we can."

*   *   *

"Mmm, that's lovely. So comforting".

Vivienne leaned back in her seat at the dressing table. She smiled at Penny who, serious of face, was concentrating on giving long, gliding brush strokes to the beautiful lengths of her silken hair.

"I'm glad it's relaxing for you, m'lady." Then, "If I might be permitted to say ..." She stilled her brushing for a moment, looking in the mirror with concern at the woman's tired face. "You seem to have been somewhat overwrought this evening."

Vivienne smiled back at this new-found treasure of hers. *Why, the girl has been here scarcely a week, but had learned so much in that time. Such a quick study, and so very sweet–"If I might be permitted to say" indeed!*

Yes, she was already picking up the oblique mode of vocal intercourse that was the standard in mistress/servant relationships. So fond of the girl had she become that she felt at this moment a sense of loss.

It would be so *good* if they could just be "Vivienne" and "Penny" to one another. Then she could pour out her woes to this girl. Just like two, equal human beings.

Ah, but no. It would not do, would not be the "Done Thing" as her mother would say.

Already, her mother had written a return to her bubbling letter of enthusiasm regarding her new "find."

Written just after Penny's hiring, though charming enough in tone on the surface, there had been a steely note of disapproval at this "precipitate move," as the Countess had put it.

Vivienne knew how much it had cost her mother that her only daughter had had to marry a man from a family in "trade."

No matter that his father had been knighted and was a wealthy man, it was, in her mother's opinion, a spurious knighthood. One given merely for his services to the economy.

The tradition for the true aristocracy had always been, of course, that titles were given for service to the king in battle–or, at the very least, in diplomacy.

The Countess had finished this letter to her daughter, with the now familiar, albeit oblique, refrain. She had hoped that the Earl and she would very soon hear some news from their daughter that would give them reason to rejoice.

A grandchild, of course. A grand*son* at that ...

She sighed, as Penny ceased her brushing. The hair lay now, a shoulder-length, shining river of chestnut with copper highlights.

"Shall I braid it for you, m'lady, for the night?"

"No, Penny dear. We'll leave it loose. My husband will be coming for a visit this evening. He likes it loose".

"Very well, m'lady."

Penny laid down the brush, seemingly the very model of discreet demureness.

Underneath this façade, however, she was seething.

She had seen, in the rare mornings following Robert's "visitations," the bruises and the tangled hair, where he had gripped and torn at it in his increasingly desperate lust.

He too, of course, was under pressure to produce a son and heir for the Hoyle Kingdom of Trade.

Like the Earl and his Countess, his own parents were beginning to wonder aloud–albeit discreetly, avoiding any sense of blame–as to when they might be informed of a "Little Miracle" in the near future.

Robert, though, was beginning to think in terms of blame. Not of himself, of course, but of his beautiful young wife. What, after all, was the use of beauty if the woman was barren?

If he wanted more beauty, he told himself, he had only to snap his fingers, and it would come running to him in droves. Well, perhaps not quite the droves that had come to him before his injuries, but sufficiently enough that his ego would be satisfied.

This very afternoon, as his wife had been coming homeward from visiting the wards–something she had begun doing recently, sensing that the men appreciated her kind intentions–her husband had appeared before her, barring her way.

At the sight of him, her face had fallen into that stupidly docile look she so often adopted these days.

He knew that underneath it all, she hated him. Well, no matter. As long as she would give him sons, he didn't give a damn what she felt.

Passing on, he had leaned briefly in and snarled, "Tonight, my lady dear, we'll make us a son–if it takes all bloody night! So, prepare yourself for me."

He then had continued on his way, limping, but with a smile of triumph on his lips.

Tonight, he'd show her. He'd be a stud *bull*, and by morning, *they would have made a son.*

Sally had surprised herself. She found that she was actually enjoying the work, and reflected that it made all the difference doing such work in the company of others. Much better, indeed, than being all alone in the house until the family had returned from their working day outside.

She and Agnes–who had asked her to call her "Aggie"–had bonded nicely. Under Aggie's tutelage, she was becoming familiar with the ins and outs of service life, and feeling more comfortable by the day.

The work was hard and constant: scrubbing floors, clearing and washing dishes, peeling vegetables and lugging, with Aggie, huge loads of laundry across the yard to the brick laundry house.

Every day, there was always laundry needing to be done. This was due to the presence of the many wounded currently occupying the house and grounds. All of this massive amount, now being done in an extension of the stables.

Once there had been horses by the dozen stabled there. Now, most of these had been taken across to the war zones. Only a very few were left, and of these, most were elderly and retired.

Much to Robert's disgust, Sir Richard had decided to let these loyal animals live on and to eventually die in peace in their own, familiar surroundings.

The space left then, by the departure of the healthy horses, had allowed this much needed expansion of laundry facilities. And the specially hired workers laboured there in shifts, from dawn until well after the onset of dusk.

Sal and Aggie were responsible for the delivery and return of not only the family laundry, but that of the officers residing on the top floor of Pembridge House.

Each day, they staggered–often giggling–with the latest pile of soiled washing for the day. At evening time, they would stagger back, having sorted, folded and checked that they were bringing back *exactly* the amount of items they had taken across that morning.

Any articles missing, and there would be complaints ...

Sally knew that Mrs. Perkins–"Mrs. B" as everyone called her, the *B* standing for "Bessie"–had been watching her progress carefully for all of her first week.

She was gratified to note that when, eventually, the housekeeper had given the slightest of nods at Aggie, Aggie, in return, had given a nod and a smile back.

She had been approved!

Also, she had begun to relax concerning her fear of being recognised, by either Robert, or Vivienne.

The upstairs life of its denizens, being almost totally divorced from the lives of those labouring downstairs, their paths rarely crossed.

On this day, however, Penny had promised that Sally would accompany Lady Vivienne and her, out to the tents, where the regular fighting men were housed.

This, at last, was her chance to see her brother George. The proviso being that he would be in a fit enough state to receive them.

Tentatively–Robert might still be there–Penny, holding the tray with Vivienne's breakfast, knocked on the bedroom door.

No gruff male voice replied, but neither did a female voice either.

With a worried frown, Penny knocked again.

"M'lady?"

This time, a small tired voice replied.

"Penny?"

Somewhat relieved, Penny opened the door and entered the room. It was dark, the curtains still drawn closed against the night.

Placing the tray carefully on the side table, she crossed the room and, after drawing the curtains wide, she turned to face the bed and her heart jolted in shocked pity for the woman lying there.

Vivienne lay with her eyes closed. Her bedclothes lying in a tangle around her. Her fists were clenched tight at her sides as though poised for a fight, and her ashen face was marred by the dark circles under her eyes, the large bruise now forming on her cheek. And–oh, dear Lord–the bloody marks around her mouth, indicating that she had been bitten.

"M'lady!"

Penny was beside the bed in two, long strides.

"Oh, *M'lady!*"

Gently, gently, she eased an arm under the limp head of her mistress.

Opening her eyes, Vivienne looked at Penny for a moment–a look that was almost triumphant. "Well," she said, her voice husky, "we'll be having a baby now. We just can't not–not after all of *that.*"

And then, her face working, she dissolved into tears, tears and small pathetic little cries like that of a broken-hearted child.

"Oh, *Vivienne!* Oh, my poor, poor girl."

All protocol forgotten, Penny took the weeping woman into her arms, rocking and crooning, crooning and rocking, until at last, the weeping began to slow, subsiding finally into a series of hiccups.

Deftly, Penny helped her up to a sitting position. Vivienne grimaced in pain and Penny, still crooning, packed the pillows around her, giving her some support.

Then, protocol remembered, she said, "I'm going down to the kitchen m'lady, and I'll pick up some nice warm water. I'll bathe you and re-make your bed with clean sheets. Oh, and I'll find some salve for your hurts. I won't be long."

Vivienne gave her a weak smile.

"Thank you, my Penny." She spoke in a whispery voice. "Thank you."

Then, her head subsiding onto the pillow. She closed her eyes in complete exhaustion, falling into her first deep sleep of the night.

Down in the kitchen, Bessie shook her head in disgust while, wide-eyed, Aggie and Sally looked on.

"Eee, that Mr. Robert! 'E's always been too big fer 'is boots, that one. Ever since 'e were just a little whippersnapper!"

Pouring water into a bowl, Penny looked over her shoulder at Sally, an apologetic smile on her face. "Sal, lovie, I don't think we're going to be seeing our George today after all. Lady Vivienne won't be well enough to go out for a day or two. I'm sorry."

Sally smiled back, nodding in understanding, and Penny's heart warmed to her. Suddenly, she was reminded of Nellie. There was, after all, a likeness there.

Her heart lurched with the missing of her friend. For the first time, after all the excitement of getting this job, of coming up to the Big House and learning the ropes, she realised how very close Nellie and she had been. They had become a real team. She wondered grimly what Nellie would have had to say at this situation.

Then, Sally was holding the door for her, Bessie was handing her some salve and promising to bring up "something really soft and easy to eat for the poor lamb" and Aggie was already sorting out clean sheets to bring up when Penny was ready.

The door closed behind her, and she did not hear Sally murmuring to herself, "Oh, Robert. You've killed her. What a *fool* of a man you are."

CHAPTER TWENTY-ONE

It was a chilly morning in April. It had rained during the night and the grass surrounding the tents was soggy.

Cilla and Nellie had just finished a shift in surgery, and now, during a lull in the action, were brewing themselves a much needed cup of tea.

"Oh, these poor men. What on earth are they going to do with themselves once they get home?" Cilla, thinking of the damage that their patients had endured, asked the question. It was a rhetorical one of course, and had been asked many times. It was also one that no one had an answer for.

"I know." Sighing, Nellie poured out the tea. "Most of them are going to be invalids for the rest of their lives."

Having poured and delivered the tea, she fingered a recent letter from home, a letter much read and pondered over ever since it had arrived. Absently running the letter through her fingers, she said, "Something should be done to help them adjust to life once they get home, but apart from their time in the convalescent hospitals, there is nothing else done for them. Their families must cope as best they can, and if they can't cope ..."

She left the sentence unfinished, for there was no solution.

"I know, m'dear, I know." Cilla reached out a comforting hand. Then asked, "How are things going with George these days?"

"Oh, somewhat better." Nellie unfurled the letter again. Then, folding it and tucking it into her apron pocket, she went on. "At first, no one except the medics were allowed near him in his wilder moods. He was just so angry. Sometimes, he had to be literally tied down, in order to prevent him from hurting either himself or others."

Cilla nodded knowingly. After all, she had been there when George had first arrived–he and the others suffering from the same angry mood swings typical of the so-called "shell shock."

"I don't know which is the worst," she said, "a terrible physical wound, that *awful* mustard gas, or the shell shock."

"I think"–Nellie was thoughtful–"I can't help feeling that with the shell shock, terrible as it is, there *must* be some way of getting them back. I wish I knew more. I really do."

She sighed again, frowning.

"Here, m'dear, let me fill your cup. Drink it up while it's still hot." Gratefully, Nellie received the proffered cup, and for a while, the pair sat in companionable silence, each of them engaged in thoughts of their own.

Penny had been keeping Nellie appraised of the news from home–good, bad and horrifying.

She had written at first of how happy she had been, settling into a job that fitted her like a glove. Lady Vivienne, she had declared, was a "sweetheart" and a most appreciative mistress.

Sally too, was doing well, making friends and proving her worth with her kitchen skills. Indeed, Mrs. B had recently declared that one day, Sally might turn into a "creditable cook." High praise indeed from the Pembridge housekeeper.

There had been no trouble with Robert, at least as far as Sally was concerned. He hadn't even noticed her in passing.

Mam and Pa had finally been allowed to see George. Even though he had been in one of his quieter moods, they had been rather distressed at the change in him, but they were dealing with it well enough. Mam had declared, "It will be what it will be, and when we get him home, things *will* get better."

Reading this, Nellie had smiled, murmuring to herself, "Oh, *Mam*, dear Mam, for your sake I do hope so."

Letters home from Will were more frequent now and, miraculously, amid all of the mayhem surrounding him, he had so far escaped without a scratch.

There had been no more news of Gareth, and Mam was comforting Alice as best she could.

Here, Nellie smiled again at the friendship that had sprung up between the two women. They were, she thought, like flowers, blooming amongst the black weeds of war.

Thinking of Gareth, Nellie felt again the familiar pang at missing Harry. There had been no news of him at all, despite the flurry of enquiries that were continuing up and down the lines.

It was almost, she thought, as though he had disappeared from the face of the earth. Her heart ached at the thought of it.

Finally, there was the news of Vivienne's pregnancy and, marring the happiness this ought to have caused her, the account of the dreadful night in which she had conceived.

Nellie had been quivering in disgust as she recounted this to Cilla. Cilla, too, had been equally horrified.

Vivienne, Penny said, had not been the same since that night. At five months gone, she was still being very sick in the mornings and was a pale, wan shadow of her former self.

The doctors, bless them, had forbidden further sexual intercourse until "matters had resolved themselves."

Far from bursting Robert's bubble, he was busily slaking his lusts on any of the willing, and there were a number, of female entities he could muster. The while, he was strutting around like a peacock. In his own mind, he was already the proud father of a bouncing baby boy.

The Earl and his Countess, Penny had gathered, were delighted, as were Sir Richard and Lady Charlotte.

The two men were oblivious to the obvious sufferings of Vivienne, putting these down as being the usual state of affairs in pregnancy. "Leave these things to the women" they said. "Her keepers will take care of her, and she will soon settle down and learn to deal with the realities of womanhood."

With that, they smilingly lit their cigars, sipped their whiskies and settled themselves comfortably back into their library chairs.

The Countess and Lady Charlotte were more concerned, but busily assuring one another that all would be well in the end. As though it would be of some comfort to themselves–a further reassurance perhaps–they had soon turned to regaling one another with tales of their own birthing woes.

"Dear Lord." At that part of the letter, Cilla had shaken her head in disgust. "Poor Vivienne, poor girl." Then, more cheerfully, "But I'm so glad she has Penny at her side at least. I'm sure she must be a great comfort to her at this time."

"Yes." Nellie was wistful. "I really miss her, though. Penny, I mean. It's like losing a limb. We'd become such good friends–and such a team."

Cilla put her arms around Nellie's shoulders in a gesture of comfort. "I miss her, too, though I'm sure not as much as you. This war just *cannot* last much longer. Since the Americans arrived, we've begun to make some progress."

Nellie nodded in agreement "They certainly are an energetic lot. A bit wild, though, from time to time!"

Cilla laughed and said, "Well, just remember where we were at this time last year. The Germans were practically on Britain's doorstep. What would have happened if we had been invaded?"

"Aye." Nellie was thoughtful. "And with Europe being entirely occupied by Germany ..."

"Where would that have left America?" Cilla sounded very definite. "At the mercy of a Germany looking to extend its empire ever further!"

Though ready to continue in this line of thought, she was interrupted by the sound of the bugle.

More wounded were arriving...

It was carnage. Truly carnage.

Accustomed as they were by now to the pitiful sights and sounds, Nellie, Cilla, Nurse Haines and the rest of the medical team, moving as fast as they could to the centre of action, were forced to catch in a collective breath at the sight before them.

Rows of men, bearers and the wounded they had been carrying, lay before them in silence. The final silence of the dead.

The only sounds to be heard were those of the living bearers who had found them. These too were mostly silent, going grim-faced about their gruesome task. Every now and then though, there would be an audible sob from one of them, quickly stifled as his companions, fighting back tears of their own, nodded in compassionate understanding.

Quickly recovering from their initial shock, the medical team set to work–sheer professionalism asserting itself.

Automatically, they separated into small groups, lifting, examin-ing, identifying where possible and organizing the living bearers into the proper mode of disposing of these sad remains. The remains of their dead comrades.

"*What happened?*" This, from Nellie, articulating the words that were on everyone's mind.

"The enemy strafed the bearers in their trenches as they were making their way here with the wounded." One of the living bearers, pausing briefly from his task, addressed the question, quickly glancing over his shoulders at the rest of the team.

There were nods and murmurs of assent from the rest of the bearers.

Nurse Haines now came bustling up. "Nellie, Cilla, take two of the other aides and organise something hot and soothing for the bearers–and a decently comfortable spot for them to sit and rest if you can."

She sighed, looking, Nellie thought, truly haggard.

"They are all in shock," Haines continued, before moving on to give instructions to another group.

As they moved to follow their instructions, Nellie glanced at Cilla. Quietly, she said, "She is in shock, too," and Cilla nodded her agreement.

They were, all of them, working flat-out when the guns started up again.

There was a momentary pause as people looked up and then back at one another, an unspoken look that said *"Dear God, what now?"* Then, it was back to work again.

The sounds of the firing came from afar at first, coming ominously nearer as the hours flew by.

Sure enough, as soon as things were on the verge of being sorted out from the current tasks, new bearers appeared, carrying even more suffering men.

The work went on ...

Later–much later–the two young women were back in their sleeping hut. Kicking off the shoes from their aching feet and detaching from themselves the aprons and belts around their waists, they fell, fully dressed, on top of their beds.

Beyond tiredness and in a state of almost catatonic unreality, yet still wired from the work they had been doing, they lay there for a short while, speechless.

"I don't think this war will *ever* end," Nellie said. "I think that we have died, and are in hell!" Now, there were tears, trickling slowly down her cheeks, unnoticed, unheeded.

"Dear heart." Cilla propped herself on one elbow. "We mustn't think that way–it will only add to this awful stress. The war *will* end. God knows when, but it *will*."

"God?" with a sudden, ferocious burst of energy Nellie, surprising even herself, flung her legs over the edge of the bed and sat, facing Cilla.

Smacking away the traitorous tears she continued, "There is no *God*. What kind of a God would allow all of ... of *this?*"

Burying her face in her hands, she began to rock, backwards and forwards, forwards and backwards, filled now with an energy that was fueled by rage.

Then, Cilla was by her side. Gently, two arms were wrapped around Nellie, arms that were filled with warmth and comfort.

"Dear, *dear* one. This war has not been created by any kind of god. It is *us*, humanity, with all our ideas of vainglory. It is our pride, our lust for power, our wilful ignorance of another's pain that fuels this conflict.

"However, this fuel is running low." Cilla was continuing with a growing certainty. "This war's momentum is deserting it. Now, for a while, we are continuing to suffer. But soon, very soon, those in power will realise that this power is empty, and war will cease, I know it."

Along with her certainty, she had been continuing to rock Nellie in her arms.

Nellie herself, soothed and comforted by these ministrations from really, a most remarkable woman, now had her head resting on Cilla's shoulder as she rocked.

Breaking free, she looked at her friend with shining eyes. "When this ends, you will be going back to the convent, yes?"

Cilla was silent for a moment. Then, smiling, she said, "Yes, yes, my dear friend. I will."

Returning the smile, Nellie said, "Yes, you belong there." Then, with a growing conviction, she added, "And one day, you will be the *best* Reverend Mother there ever was."

Then, both laughing, they turned to their pillows, and the blessings of sleep.

CHAPTER TWENTY-TWO

"Mrs. B!"

Penny came bursting through the kitchen door "It's started!"

At the momentarily startled look on the housekeeper's face–
Penny never usually rushed like this–she explained, "The pains,
they've started, and her water has broken ..."

"Well, thank the Lord for that! Perhaps the poor soul will feel
better after this." Mrs. B had already begun drawing water at the
sink pump, so it would be ready to set on the stove in case of need.

Now she called, "Sally! Aggie! You're needed. Come quick! Look
sharp about it."

Then, turning to Penny, she said, "I'll send one to fetch a doctor
and nurse, the other to warn Lady Charlotte. You go now, m'dear.
I'm sure the poor girl needs your comfort."

Pausing only to say, "We've got to keep Mr. Robert away from
her–at all costs," Penny opened the kitchen door just as Aggie and
Sally came rushing in.

Not stopping to speak to them, she nodded briefly as she moved
past. Explanations could be left to Mrs. B.

Upstairs, Vivienne greeted her, gasping for air. Penny could see
that she was not only in pain, but terrified.

Wringing out a flannel in cold water from the ewer, she placed
it on Vivienne's forehead, then set about giving what comfort
she could.

She was, of course, thoroughly used to comforting wounded and dying men. However, in this case, though the terror and the pain were the same, the circumstances were somewhat different. How she wished that she had been given at least a modicum of midwifery training at Camberwell. But of course, there had been no call for that at the Front.

She had, on her days off, and as Vivienne's difficult pregnancy had progressed, garnered some small information from Alice. Her mam, anticipating the possibility of an early delivery, had given her some small information as to what to expect as the baby emerged.

As for the afterbirth, Alice had said, "Leave that to the midwife, lovie–she'll know what to do."

Of course, Sir Richard had ordered a specialist from Leeds to come up to Eldenfield for the birth, and he would have been accompanied by an experienced midwife.

Two rooms had been reserved for the lengths of their stay, and all was set for their arrival next week.

Plenty of time, it had been thought, for them to be on hand for the birth. The baby, however, had had other ideas and now was coming early.

Vivienne was now grunting with the force of her baby's determination to sever from her.

She herself, though, seemed to be rapidly weakening, and Penny was frantic with worry.

Oh, why don't they come?

As if anticipating this thought, the door opened and Lady Charlotte glided in. She was followed by a doctor who had been hastily co-opted from the wards. He was followed by two nurses.

Penny and Lady Charlotte now exchanged glances. Penny could see that her worry was being reflected back to her.

Moving aside to make way for the professionals to get to work, the two women waited in suspense for the eventual outcome.

Mrs. B now came bustling in with a large jug of hot water, which she placed on the side table ready for use. Then, after laying down soap and warmed towels, she turned to look at the woman struggling in labour and her hand flew to her mouth, stifling a gasp.

Lady Charlotte jerked her head in dismissal. Giving a small, apologetic bob, the housekeeper left the room.

Penny could see, briefly, as the door opened and then closed during the older woman's exit, that a small group of servants, well-wishers all, were gathered outside. All of them agog for news.

The nurses were now pulling the top bedclothes away from Vivienne, leaving her body, legs akimbo, ready for the delivery.

She was as white as the sheets themselves, her face and body ashen with sweat. The groans were coming faster now, with scarcely any let-up between them. Penny ached with longing to comfort her.

As they watched, a tiny head emerged, crowning through the now-gaping vaginal exit. Then, with one, long, roar of effort from the mother, the baby slipped effortlessly into the waiting towel held by one of the nurses.

She was a perfect baby girl. All hands, feet, fingers and toes intact. The lungs were obviously in fine condition, too, for the room was filled, suddenly, with loud and lusty cries.

As the nurse moved away from the bed in order to wash and wrap the child, Penny, with a quick *"May I?"* glance at Lady Charlotte, moved to help with the cleansing and ordering of her mistress.

Just as she reached the bed, there came a huge contraction from Vivienne, and suddenly the bed was a flood of red.

With a curse, the doctor grabbed at the pile of towels and began to struggle in vain to stem the flow.

The room was suddenly silent. Even the baby had ceased from crying and was now breathing quietly, comfortably wrapped as she was.

Penny leaped to Vivienne's side. Pushing away the doctor's arms as he sought to restrain her, she took the young mother's head into her embrace.

All protocol forgotten, she murmured, over and over again, "Oh Vivienne, my poor, darling girl. Oh, sweet Vivienne!"

Weakly, Vivienne opened her eyes and smiled. "Penny". It was a whisper, then "Boy?"

"Yes."

There was a sharp intake of breath from Lady Charlotte. Ignoring this, Penny, determined to give some last comfort repeated, "Yes, Vivienne, you have given us a fine boy. He's lovely."

"Oh." Vivienne smiled, adding weakly, "Papa will be so pleased."

And she was gone.

The funeral was a simple affair. The ballroom at Pembridge House was magnificently decked out in lilies and the exquisite white roses from the corner of the garden not in use for hospital purposes.

Vivienne had loved these roses, and Lady Charlotte, remembering this, had made sure they were included in the decorations.

The local vicar was conducting the service, and the ballroom was packed with sorrowing well-wishers–servants, off-duty nurses and medics–many of them openly weeping.

Penny, stiff with repressed anger, was standing, alongside Mrs. B, Sally and Aggie, at the head of most of both the inside and outside Pembridge workforce.

Conspicuous for his absence was the Earl of Marchmont. His Countess was there, though, looking worn and sad. She had seen her granddaughter and, eyes filled with tears had kissed her and given her a blessing.

Just before the service was ready to begin, Lady Charlotte moved across to where Penny was standing, her fists clenched, as she fought for control over the few tears that were still unshed.

"My dear, I would be most grateful if, once the service is ended, you would follow myself, the Countess and Sir Richard upstairs to the nursery. As you know, the vicar has kindly consented to move from sorrow into joy. Our little girl is to be baptised."

Dumbly, Penny nodded, giving a curtsey that was just a speck deeper than the curt little bob required of a serving girl.

Noting this, Charlotte smiled to herself. *Yes, she had style, this young woman. She would do nicely.*

"And Mr. Robert?" Penny was working hard to keep the disgust out of her voice. The wretched man was nowhere to be seen.

A shadow crossed his mother's face as she replied, tight-lipped, "His father has spoken to him. He won't be here today–not for the funeral service, nor yet the baptism."

There was a loud "Ahem" from the vicar, and someone began to play a sweet melody on the grand piano. The service was about to begin.

As the melody swelled, four young men entered, carrying the casket on their broad shoulders.

Penny could hardly bear the thought of those sad remains, now held aloft by these young men. She spent the entire length of the short, but solemn service, biting her lip and staring stolidly out of the window.

Then, it was over. The casket was being carried out of the ballroom, down to the grand entrance hall and from thence, out through the oaken double doors to the sweeping driveway.

There, the funeral cortege waited while the casket was loaded, ready to be taken, along with the Countess, back to Marchmont Castle.

Once there, Vivienne, the last of her line, would join her ancestors in the family vault.

But first, there was a baptism to be accomplished, so while most of the servants, nurses and others dispersed to take up their regular duties, Penny, along with Lady Charlotte, Sir Richard, the Countess and the vicar, as well as the doughty Mrs. B., mounted the grand staircase. There, the latest Hoyle was waiting, unawares, to be baptised.

The blue paint of the nursery–prepared for a boy–had been hastily repainted pink, and the room was now considered suitable for the girl who would be spending much of her early life here.

The smell of fresh paint was currently being dealt with by the large windows, now open to the summer sunshine and the scent of newly cut grass.

The vicar, now in less sombre mood, was pouring a stream of water gently over the forehead of the child.

"In the name of the Father, the Son, and the Holy Ghost, I baptise thee Elizabeth"–here, the Countess nodded graciously in the direction of Lady Charlotte for allowing the use of her name to be the first–"Charlotte Vivienne. Amen."

Now, there was a chorus of "Amens" from the assembled group, and they began to smile at one another.

"She has been well-named, m'dears." Sir Richard looked around the small group of attendees, beaming in jovial satisfaction.

Then, at the slightest shake of his wife's head, he immediately sobered, remembering what else had just transpired.

Penny could feel the suppressed shake of laughter from Mrs. B, standing beside her. Even she could not help but smile, at this oh-so human interaction between husband and wife.

Leaving the room now, the baby safely left in the care of her wet nurse, the group gathered again at the top of the grand staircase.

Finding Sally and Aggie lurking shamefacedly outside the room, Mrs. B wagged a finger at them, then chivied them towards the back stairs leading down to the kitchens.

Momentarily hesitating, the housekeeper looked first towards Penny, then at Lady Charlotte. Shaking her head briefly, Charlotte touched Penny's arm in an indication that she was to accompany the formal group downstairs.

Satisfied, and with a quick "C'm along, young lasses–there's work to be done," Mrs. B. and the two young maidservants departed in the opposite direction, Sally directing a quick look at Penny that was one big question mark.

Penny shook her head, indicating that she, too, was puzzled.

Reluctantly, Sally followed the other two through the green baize doors that led to the back of the house.

Sir Richard and the vicar descended with the rest of the party trailing behind them–Penny at the rear. Her heart was pounding. She feared that soon, Lady Charlotte would take her aside and tell her that her services were no longer required.

At this thought, she was suddenly overwhelmed with a feeling of bitterness that she found hard to suppress.

As they emerged from the house, the June sunshine smiled a benediction upon the small band and upon those of the cortege, who had been faithfully waiting for the last hour or so.

There was a hasty rolling down of shirtsleeves and a donning of sober black jackets. This, along with a resumption of the solemn expressions, thought to be suitable for the occasion.

The vicar, with a final bow and a "God bless you all," mounted his bicycle, then wobbled his way down the driveway.

Engines were started, Lady Charlotte and the Countess Elizabeth engaged in a brief embrace. Then Sir Richard, bowing, took Elizabeth's hand. He kissed it and, before releasing it, gave it a gentle squeeze–a mute declaration of solidarity.

"Please do feel that you may come and see your granddaughter as many times as you wish" he said. This sentiment was echoed in a quick smile, and a wave from Charlotte.

The chauffer respectfully helped his illustrious passenger into the seat beside him. Gently, he closed the door before settling himself into the driving seat.

The two funeral officials were seated behind, keeping watch over their precious charge for the journey home.

The engine revs increased, and the hearse moved forward, slowly at first, and then increasing speed as it swooped down the driveway.

Richard and Charlotte waved until it disappeared around the bend. Then, sighing, the couple looked at one another. Both knew the sourness that Elizabeth would be returning to. The Earl had made it clear that both his late daughter and her offspring had, for him, simply ceased to exist.

Shaking himself out of this mood, Sir Richard clapped his hands together with a brisk "Well, I'll be off back to my duties."

With the slightest of nods in Penny's direction, he gave his wife a meaningful look. She returned this with an affectionately amused nod. Then he was gone, striding off in the direction of the stables.

Now, Penny was alone with Lady Charlotte.

"Well, Penny dear, we must have a talk." *Here it comes,* Penny thought to herself. She braced for the blow.

"Come, we will have tea sent up to my quarters."

Charlotte extended her arm in the direction of the doorway.

Reluctantly, Penny followed her through the entrance hall, and once again, up the grand staircase to the cozy room that Charlotte called her "office."

Ringing the bell for tea, Lady Charlotte indicated to Penny that she should sit. Obediently, Penny obeyed. She couldn't stop herself from wondering, however, just how many people had been hired–and fired–in this very room.

Soon, Aggie appeared, bearing tea, scones and cakes for two. Mrs. B had anticipated that these might soon be called for.

She also, sensible soul, had sent Aggie with the tray rather than Sally, knowing how difficult it might be for both her and Penny to have to play the role of servant for a friend ...

Smilingly, Charlotte poured the tea, indicating that Penny should take a scone, as she herself now proceeded to do.

Remembering the first time that tea had been taken at Pembridge House–oh, how *long* ago that seemed now–Penny was almost on the verge of tears. Dutifully, however, she took a scone and began to butter it.

Charlotte was now happily munching. There had not been much time for eating on this busy, emotionally charged day. Penny, on the other hand, put the smallest crumb in her mouth and almost choked on it. Hastily, she took a gulp of tea before crumbling the rest into pieces on her plate.

"Now, my dear." Charlotte, having finished her mouthful and taken a long sip of tea, was preparing to get down to business.

Penny could stand it no longer. "Oh, Lady Charlotte–m'lady–please, *please* don't send me away! I'll do *anything* to stay here. I love this place. I'll work among the men as I'm trained to do. You do remember that, m'lady, don't you? I'm a trained Red Cross nurse ... I ..."

She got no further. Suddenly, Charlotte was beside her, holding her hands and apologising profusely. "Oh, my *dear*, poor girl. Sending you away is the *last* thing on my mind. Rather, Sir Richard and I have been discussing the possibility of offering you an alternative role here. Oh my dear, I'm so sorry. How careless of me not to have noticed your distress earlier."

Fumbling in the pocket of her gown, Charlotte brought out a flimsy, pretty apology for a handkerchief and pressed it upon Penny. "You can bring it back at any time." She smiled when Penny demurred.

Taking the handkerchief, Penny delicately turned her head away in order to blow. Charlotte, laughing delightedly at this display of delicate feeling, resumed her seat.

Indicating the tasty display in front of them, she said, "Now, child. Eat, drink, and while you do so, I will explain myself in full."

Lady Charlotte, whilst informing Penny of the bare fact that Sir Richard had forbidden his son to attend the funeral, had failed to fill her in with the *full* facts of the matter.

Sir Richard had indeed spoken to Robert–informing him in no uncertain terms that he would not be welcome, not only for the duration of the mourning period, but for an indefinite period of at least several months following.

He was to be shipped off to his uncle's place in Scotland, there to dwell upon his appallingly bad behaviour, and to make, if he could, some reparation for his sins.

This did not sit well with Robert.

"But *Father*, the place is a bloody *farm*. I've hardly ever met Uncle Malcolm, and when I have, he's hardly struck me as being a friendly sort."

"That's because you were not being exactly friendly yourself as I remember. It takes two to tango, don't y'know?"

"But, what will I *do* there. There's nobody around that suits my sort. Aunt Maggie is dour in the extreme. I never got on with her either. The place is miles away from civilisation of any kind–surrounded by bloody bog and heather. The weather's appalling and there's not even a *pub!*"

"Nor," his father parried, with a trace of a smile, "are there any bonnie lasses, hmm?"

"No, there are not! *Pa* ..." Robert was wheedling now. "What am I to *do* there–all there is, is milking bloody cows and ploughing and *stuff!*"

"Yes, my boy–and that is exactly what you will be doing. You will be a great help to your uncle now that he is aging. He'll see to that. He promised me".

Robert was aghast. "I won't. I won't do that sort of mucky work. That's for peons, not for gentlemen."

"I see. You regard yourself as a gentleman, do you?" Sir Richard was now quivering with rage himself. "A *gentleman* bullies his young wife into ill health, does he? No, *sir*. You are no gentleman. I'm not quite sure what your mother and I thought we were doing when we gave you the education of a gentleman, but all I can see before me now is an ignorant, spoiled, bullying brat!

"I'm disgusted with your behaviour, *sir–you* are no more than the 'peon' that you so despise. You will go, and you will do the peon's work and be glad for it!"

Robert now drew himself up with all of the remnants of dignity he could muster. "No sir, I will *not* go, and you cannot force this upon me."

He turned to leave, but Sir Richard, his voice like ice, said quietly, "Then you can go elsewhere–wherever you please, to work at the mill if you wish. But you will never set foot in this house again, and you will never receive a single penny from me. That's it, sir. Take it, or leave it."

Robert left that day for Scotland.

*　　*　　*

"What happened?"

"What did she say?"

A chorus of young voices gathered around Penny as she entered the kitchen - while Mrs. B brandished a rolling pin in mock battle mode. "Off y'go, lassies. To yer duties. *Now!*"

Reluctantly, the young maid servants scattered to their work.

Seeing Sally's expression of dismay, the housekeeper added, "No, Sally. Y'cn stay to talk to your friend. Here–" She indicated a corner of the kitchen table that was, for the moment at least, not covered in preparations for the evening meal.

"Mind, though, the both of you've to be back at your duties in just minutes," and with that, she retired to her end of the long table and, a knowing smile upon her face, continued with her kneading.

The pair sat down at their corner–Penny, obviously pent-up with a tale to tell, Sally, agog for the telling.

"Tell, Penny. It doesn't look as if you have to leave, so *tell*."

Penny took in a deep breath, then said, "Well, I was sure that I was going to have to leave, that there wouldn't be a place for me here anymore." She paused for a moment, living once again the loss of Vivienne.

Sally, understanding, reached out and squeezed her hand then, prompting, "So, you have a new position? *Tell*."

"I do. Oh, Sal–I *do*! Lady Charlotte has offered me the charge of Vivienne's baby, little Elizabeth. I can hardly believe it, but it's true."

At her end of the table, Mrs. B nodded to herself in quiet satisfaction. *A very good move,* she was thinking. *The girl is an excellent choice.*

"Oh, *my!* Wait until we tell our mams–they'll be that *pleased!*" Sally was squirming again, this time in delight. "So, what did m'lady *say* exactly?"

"Well–" Penny took another deep breath. She could hardly believe it herself. "She said that she had been watching the way I cared for Viv–for Lady Vivienne."

Once again, Mrs. B nodded in approval at this return to protocol.

"And, though I have no formal training as a nanny, she feels that my Red Cross training will stand me in good stead."

Sally nodded in agreement at this, and Mrs. B, busy now splitting the dough into two pans for the rising, was pleased at this sign of friendship between the two young women.

"Of course," Penny continued, "for the moment, the wet nurse will be filling most of little Elizabeth's needs, but I will be overseeing how things are done, and the baby and I will be getting to know one another in the meantime."

Now, both Sally and Mrs. B were nodding at this. "And then, in a few months' time, when she is weaned, I will have sole charge of her care."

There was a warning "Time's up" sound coming now from Mrs. B, and Sally, rising, bent to give this friend of her sister's a hug of congratulation. Mrs. B, still smiling, handed the two pans of dough to her. She moved to take them to the pantry, where they could rise until they were ready for the oven.

Standing for a moment with the pans in her hand, Sally said, "I'm so pleased for you, Penny. And our Nell will be thrilled at the news."

Penny, had risen now, too. "Thank you, Mrs. B. I'm going up now to see what might be needing to be done."

"You are most welcome, m'dear, and many congratulations from all of us down here."

Smiling, wiping her floury hands on a tea cloth, she approached Penny, giving her a quick hug before opening the door for her.

Making her way slowly up the back stairs, Penny pondered upon what else Lady Charlotte had told her.

She had spoken of her son, Robert. He had been born at just about the time when Richard Hoyle had been in the process of amassing his fortune.

The child had been born seemingly healthy, but over the months following his birth, this health had declined. He had contracted an attack of the dreaded pertussis, the "whooping cough."

Charlotte had spent sleepless days and nights stroking the child and calming him, as he whooped and choked. His fever had been high, and he had struggled for breath.

Much to the doctor's surprise, he had eventually recovered--albeit remaining frail for many months.

"After that," Lady Charlotte had said, "there was nothing, we felt, that would be good enough for him. He had the best of every-thing–particularly as our fortunes increased. He had the best of care, the best educational opportunities, his own ponies, and later, horses. Everything, everything. He had only to ask and it would be given to him.

"It was only later," she had continued, "that we began to realise how much of a mistake we had made. And by then it was too late ..."

She had paused for a moment, considering. Then finally, deciding that she would trust Penny completely. "We discovered that he had an uncontrollable temper and that this, coupled with an entirely unwarranted sense of entitlement, was turning him into"–here she had sighed–"a most unpleasant young man."

Wondering if perhaps she had maybe gone too far, she had paused, looking at Penny somewhat quizzically.

Gently, Penny had said, "Lady Charlotte, I do understand that you have been kind enough to honour me with your confidence. I will not disclose any of this to anyone else. I promise."

Gratefully, Charlotte had taken Penny's hands in hers, thinking to herself that, indeed, this young person was a most excellent choice for the task she had been given.

Thoughtfully, Penny made her way now to the nursery. Standing for a moment, she savoured the thought of this new position of hers. Of the years to come, where she would love and guide this child of Vivienne's, would give her the love and care that would have been her mother's task if she had lived.

Now, taking a deep breath, she knocked on the door and entered.

CHAPTER TWENTY-THREE

It Is Ended

November 11, 1918

Stunned almost to disbelief, the people were slowly beginning to realise that the world had changed. The war had ended. It was over.

On the surface of things, there was joy. Young ones–especially those who had remained relatively untouched by what had been going on during the last four years, those who had been too young to join the fray, whose families had escaped the loss of any of their members–were celebrating.

The celebrations were on the surface, however. The fireworks, the bands, the waving of flags, the triumphantly pompous messages on radio and in the newspapers, meant little to the vast undertow of the nation.

Those who had lost their loved ones, those who had come home with severed limbs, were eyeless, or who had been made mad by poisonous gas or by sheer trauma ... These did not celebrate.

These are they who now say, along with their families, "Won? What have we won?" and "What have we *lost*?"

Home!

Following their docking at Dover, Nellie and Cilla were met by two Sisters of the Holy Family, Cilla's order.

One of the sisters, quite elderly, was seated in style at the back of the Riley. The other, younger sister, was driving–a look of grim concentration on her face.

Upon seeing the two young women, however, their faces relaxed into beaming smiles. The car came to a grinding halt–the driver, in her excitement, having hit both pedal and brake at the same moment. The passenger sister clucked disapprovingly, while the driver flushed guiltily. At this, Cilla snorted with suppressed laughter. This was hastily checked, while Nellie, smiling herself, looked on in fascination.

Soon, the two sisters were out of the car and heading towards their target. "Oh, Cilla, *darling!*" the younger one was bubbling with excitement. Reaching Cilla, she threw her arms around the returning prodigal, hugging her fiercely–a hug that Cilla returned with warmth.

The older sister approached with decorum, pronouncing in stern tones as she did so, "*Really* Sister Hilda, remember where you are!" There was, however, a twinkle in her eye as she too, took Cilla into a warm embrace.

Then, turning to Nellie she said, "And this young lady is?"

"Oh, Sister Frances, please meet my dear friend and comrade in arms, Nellie. Nellie Parkin."

Holding out a hand, Sister Frances glided towards Nellie with great dignity. "Very glad to meet you, Miss Parkin. We have been hearing some very good things about you."

Nellie, resisting an instinctive urge to curtsey, took the proffered hand of this dignified woman and, with the slightest of bows, said, "I'm pleased to meet you Sister Frances". Then, looking across to Sister Hilda, she added, "And you too, sister."

"Oh, yes. Yes *indeed*–quite lovely, my dear child." Her headlong rush towards Nellie, showing every intention of hugging her too, was stopped by a harrumph from the older woman, still, however, with a twinkle in her eye.

Soon, they were all settled into the Riley. Sisters at the front, Nellie and Cilla in the back.

Sister Frances, taking a look at Nellie's luggage, and noting the tiredness in her face, declared that they must, of course, drive her to the station and deposit her there, before continuing on their journey home.

Tired as she was, Nellie gratefully accepted.

Once arrived at the station, she prepared to disembark, but Cilla, overcome with emotion at this final farewell, hugged her fiercely, while Sister Frances pretended not to see.

"Goodbye, my dear friend," Cilla whispered. "All the very best, and I shall pray nightly that you and Harry might meet again soon."

The car jerked into action, gears grinding. Sister Frances was looking exasperated, while Sister Hilda, biting her lip in furious concentration, focussed with all of her might on this highly complicated activity called "driving."

Cilla, the while, was suppressing both tears and giggles simultaneously, hands up to her face in order to disguise all signs of emotion.

Nellie stood and watched sadly, as one of the two best friends she had ever known–the other, of course, being Penny–left her to begin an entirely different kind of life than Nellie would ever know.

The Riley, still jerking, disappeared around a corner, and was gone.

Picking up her bags, Nellie turned towards her train, already waiting at the platform.

Hours later, she alighted at Eldenfield, and there was Pa, ready and waiting to take his daughter back into his arms once more.

She slept for two days and two nights, waking on Sunday morning to find Mam gently shaking her shoulder.

"Wake now, our Nell. There's a good lass. I've brought you up a jug of hot water for y'to wash thysen, *and* I'm making eggs and bacon for breakfast." This was said with enormous pride. "So don't be taking too long in comin' down."

Then, briefly kissing her daughter's forehead, Mam added, "Welcome home, our Nell. *Welcome* home".

Ten minutes later and halfway down the stairs, the aromatic scents wafting up to meet her assailed Nellie's nose, and it twitched in happy anticipation.

"How did you manage this, Mam? Eggs and bacon–we've *never* been able to eat like this before." Then, the light dawning, she said, "Oh yes, Sally?"

"Aye." Mam beamed as Pa, eating heartily himself, chuckled softly.

"Aye," Mam repeated. "It's comin' back to ye then. Y'were that tired when y'got home." With a small grunt she added, "And small wonder, considering what y've been through these last years!" Mam reached out to touch her daughter gently on the cheek, while Pa watched in satisfaction at this moment of tenderness.

When they had finished eating, Mam picked up the dishes, neatly piling them into a tidy heap.

As Nellie moved to help, Mam held out her arm to stop her. "Nay, lass, not today. Not until y'are properly mended. Pa, would y'be so kind as to make us a nice cuppa tea?"

Smiling, Pa, in a perfect imitation of butlerhood bowed. "Yes, Ma'am. Is there anything else you'd be wanting, m'lady?" And they all laughed.

With the two women settled once more at the table, steaming cups before them, Pa excused himself. Then he was off to the back-yard to do his usual Sunday morning "tinkering."

Mam began, "Well now, lovie. Things seem to be turning t'the better now, at last." Nellie, taking a sip of hot liquid, nodded in agreement. "We've had a letter from our Will and he is good and safe. They'll be keeping him, he says, for a short while longer before he's demobbed. A "mopping up" operation he says, whatever that might be."

Again, Nellie nodded. She took a thoughtful sip and wondered, given the terrain over there, exactly how safe, or not safe, things might be. She said nothing of this to her mother, however, merely murmuring, "It'll be lovely having him home again."

"Aye." Mam beamed, then said, "O'course we told you about our George the night y'come back. D'yer remember?"

"Aye." Nellie was amused to find herself reverting to the Eldenfield dialect. "I remember. He is staying on at Pembridge House as part of a medical study. I remember you telling me that."

"Aye." Mam picked up her thread. "Sir Richard, bless his heart, has become fascinated by this problem of so many men coming home suffering from the 'shell shock.' That's what they call it."

Nellie nodded as Mam continued. "So George, having it real bad." Her brow darkened for a moment, but then she swallowed hard and went on. "Well, he is one of about six or seven men chosen by the hospital ..." Again, a dark memory, that of Sally's experience, intervened.

Nellie reached out and clasped her mother's hand. Mam, recovering, went on. "Sir Richard and Lady Charlotte seem to be happy to give over nearly half of Pembridge House to the patients and hospital staff. It's to be called the Marchmont Wing after that poor lass that died."

She tailed off again for a moment, before picking up the thread. "So George can come home every other Sunday for the day, but then has to go back for his treatments. He won't say what they do to him." She heaved a sigh, shaking her head. "But he *does* seem to be improving." Then, with honesty, she added, "Well, he goes up and down, y'know, and yer never quite sure how y'will find him." Again she shook her head, clearly not knowing quite what to think.

Nellie tightened her grasp. She knew all too well what her mother was struggling to express–and also all too well that, for the moment at least, there did not seem to be a solution to the problem. She wished with all her heart that these medical interventions would help her poor brother and all those who were suffering in like fashion. However, having seen what she had seen, her hopes were limited.

Giving her mother's hand a gentle shake before releasing it, she said, "Well, I do hope to see for myself how he's doing. I suppose, though, I'll have to wait until next Sunday."

Before Mam could reply to this, there was a knocking at the door. "Oh, lovie." Mam started up from her chair. "That's likely Penny. I forgot. It's her Sunday off and she hoped to come and see you."

Hurriedly, she moved to the door and opened it. There Penny stood, flushed with eagerness and, seeing Nellie, she beamed in delight.

The two friends, each one rushing to meet the other, collided with one another in the middle of the room. Both of them now bursting with laughter while they hugged. Each one outdoing the other with enthusiastic greetings, until the inevitable tears began to flow.

Tactfully, Mam removed herself from their space. Out through the backdoor to the yard, smiling to herself, she went to join with Pa in his "tinkering."

As they began to recover from the tears, Penny, noticing the sudden absence of Mam and Pa, exclaimed, "Eh, Nell. Your poor mam and your pa! They must be out in the back. It's *freezing* out there. Let's go for a walk. Ooh, I've got so much to tell you!"

Flinging on a heavy scarf and climbing into her boots, Nellie said, "Aye, and me too. But first, you must tell me all about what's going on at Pembridge House. How are you doing there? And how is George? And baby Elizabeth? And Sally?"

Laughing, Penny said "*C'mon,* our Nell! I'll tell you all about it while we walk. Now, *please* call your parents in before we go. 'Tisn't fair to keep 'em out of a nice warm kitchen on a cold November day like this. Not just for the sake of tact at any rate."

*   *   *

The two young women were in one of their favourite walking spots, the canal. Penny had seemed full of suppressed excitement while they'd been making their way down the hill to the tow path, and the pair had been talking "nineteen to the dozen" as Mam would say. Penny, however, had not yet imparted any important news, and was obviously hugging something to herself in gleeful anticipation of a revelation yet to come.

Nellie, faintly amused, was waiting patiently for this good friend of hers to come clean. In the meantime, Penny touched briefly on the subject of George. She told Nellie that he was as well as could be expected, but that there was still a long journey of healing ahead of him, if indeed, healing would be possible. Nellie, only too familiar with the hazards of shock, nodded gravely. Penny squeezed briefly at her shoulder, a comforting gesture.

He was, however, she had continued, really looking forward to seeing his sister again. "Aye, me too," Nellie murmured.

"And"–Penny brightened–"Elizabeth is just lovely and healthy as could be–a darling child."

Sally too was doing really well. She had settled in nicely. And was getting to be "*ever* such a good cook."

Grinning mischievously, Penny added, "And that young Billy just dotes on her. We can all see that–plain as the nose on our faces. Sal won't hear of it of course, but ... well, time will tell. Time will tell."

Matchmaking ended, though, she saddened. "We've not yet heard from our Gary, and we don't yet know if he's even alive. But, me mam lives in hopes. Always"

Now it was Nellie's turn to comfort. Reaching out, she touched her friend's hand in sympathy. "I've a real soft spot for your mam," she said, remembering how Alice had encouraged her to reach for better things.

"I know, and she for you. Believe me, Nell."

Linking arms, the pair walked on. Nellie could sense that Penny had something she wanted to impart, but also that for some reason she seemed to be holding back. Perhaps, she thought, she was waiting for the right moment, and so decided to allow her to take her time.

Still linked, they walked on for a while in companionable silence.

Except for the ever-present seagulls, wheeling and shrieking above them, the place was deserted. No busy bargemen, and no barges. Just the wind blowing tiny wavelets that rippled along the surface of the waters.

It was beginning to get really cold, the early darkness coming on. Away on the other side of the canal, they could see the street lamps coming alive under the careful hands of the lamplighters.

Well, if Penny is holding something back–and she really did seem to be seething with controlled excitement–*I'd better initiate the conversation myself,* Nellie thought.

She was just about to speak when Penny, relinquishing her hold, turned to face her. "And what sort of work were you thinking of taking up now that you are back, our Nell?"

Nellie felt the world shifting under her. *This is it? Is this all that Penny has to say?* Abruptly, she turned away, moving swiftly back along the path that they had come.

Penny, puzzled, followed her, while Nellie increased her pace. Catching up with her friend, Penny grabbed at her arm. She was quite honestly puzzled.

Nellie pulled away and, almost spitting out the words, said, "To answer your stupid question–it'll probably be back at the mill, *if* they'll have me." She turned away once more. She was striding so fast that she was now almost running down the frost-hardened towpath.

"No–*no, Nellie!*" Horrified at the miscalculation she had made of her friend's mood, Penny also began to run.

Heaving her shawl around herself against the growing cold, she hurled herself down the path in pursuit of this dearest of her friends. She *had to* make amends ...

Nellie, refusing to acknowledge the desperate pleas coming from behind her, continued on at a precipitate pace, her nose firmly in the air. It suddenly occurred to her that that she had not behaved in this manner since infant school. She began to slow her pace.

In that instant, an errant seagull shrieked down upon her. He was diving straight for her hat, obviously thinking that it might be edible.

Stupid bird, she thought. Taking off the hat, she flapped it at him with furious energy. Affronted, he rose into the air. Circling her head just once, he screeched outraged seagull imprecations at her, while the rest of the gathering crowd of birds joined in automatically.

Suddenly amused, Nellie found herself wondering if they were supposing that this strange, flapping woman was posing some threat of danger.

By the time that Penny, puffing and full of half-phrased apologies, caught up with her, Nellie's anger and incipient tears had turned to laughter.

Then, the pair were in each other's arms. Both of them trying to apologise at once, and both of them laughing heartily.

The seagulls, after doing one more turn about their heads, left in disgust. As they flew, they cawed in protest at this missed chance at nourishment.

By now, the two young women were sufficiently recovered as to become coherent. Penny seized her chance to explain. "Oh Nell, I'm so sorry. I was just teasing you when I asked that stupid question. Of *course* you won't be going back to the mill–and not just because they wouldn't have you.

"No, there is a far better job just waiting for you up at the house– and Lady Charlotte is asking you to fill it!"

Mam, Pa, Alice and daughter Izzie – along with Penny and Nell, were finishing their supper at the Nanton Street house.

Supper had been served early. "Well," Mam had said, handing round the plates. "Even though breakfast were late, Penny has to get back to the house for work tomorrow, so she mustn't miss the last tram back! Will that young man, the gardener, be meetin' you at t'stop then, lass?"

Mouth full, Penny nodded and swallowed. "Aye, Mrs. Parkin," she said. "He's a faithful sort is our Billy."

Nellie, laughing, said "Why, is he courting you, our Penn?"

"Nay, not *me*". Penny looked meaningfully around the table, and everyone laughed, waiting expectantly for some further revelation. Penny, however, said no more.

"Oh, Aye." Alice spoke out. "The lad's but a wee sprat of a thing– far too young to think about doin' any courtin'."

Mam nodded in agreement, and Nellie was amused at the under-current of thought that the two woman were sharing. *"And not nearly good enough for one of our girls ..."*

She could see that Pa had also noted this unspoken exchange, and that he, like Nellie, was amused.

When the two girls had arrived home from their walk, everyone had already been there, waiting for their return. Alice and Nellie had embraced like the two good friends that they were, albeit from different generations.

"Eee, *lass!* Eee, it's good to see you!" She had held Nellie away from her, regarding her intently before nodding to herself. "Aye, Penny were the same," she murmured quietly. "Y'all need fattening up. Just like she did."

Out of the corner of her eye, Nellie watched as Penny, simulating indignation, patted her neat, slim stomach.

Alice, however, was serious. "This has been a *dreadful* war–and there's many a one that'll never get over it."

Watching her mother's face contracting in pain, Nellie thought, *She's thinking of our George.*

Pa had come to the rescue with "Well now, ladies, talking of fattening up, I would like to say it's time we started on this lovely meal."

The tension broken, and with everyone laughing and chattering, they sat down, waiting before starting to eat, until Mam and Alice had finished serving and had joined them at the table.

"Well, now." Alice turned to Nellie beside her. "I'm sure that our Penny has given you the good news?"

Nellie, unable to resist teasing her friend replied with "Aye, *eventually* she's managed to get around to it".

Penny pretended to blush, making a self-deprecating gesture as she did so. Nellie smiled forgivingly, a twinkle in her eye.

"Aye." Mam beamed. "We were that pleased to hear about it when Penny told us."

"Huh!" Nellie continued to tease, then relenting, she reached over and grasped Penny's hand. "I'm *so* pleased. I can't thank you enough for mentioning me to Lady Charlotte."

Penny smiled "Well, to be honest about it, it was *she* who mentioned you to *me*. We were talking about how sad it was that nothing much could be done for these poor men."

Again, Nellie noticed a moment of darkness on Mam's brow, but it cleared almost instantly as she said, "Well, I'm sure Penny, lovie, t'was *you* what put the thought into her head. Putting two and two together like."

Smiling, Penny nodded in acknowledgement. "Well, yes. As soon as she realised that Nell and Sally were sisters, and that George was their brother–and also understanding that you and I, Nell, had both trained as nursing assistants *and* had experience overseas–well, it was *she* that put two and two together in the end. In fact, she told me that if you were as good a worker as our Sally, you would be very good indeed."

Mam, Pa and Alice all beamed at this. "Aye," Mam declared, "and hasn't our Sal just turned out to be great at what she does!"

"Aye, Mrs. Parkin. Mrs. B has taken to calling her, her treasure," Penny added, "and coming from Mrs. B, that's quite a compliment."

Not to be outdone, Alice chimed in with "And now our Isobel." She smiled fondly at her younger daughter. "Our Izzie, working where our Penny used to–at Brombridges. Really, don't you all think that things are beginning to look up a bit, after all we've been through?"

Everyone cheered in agreement and then, the ancient kitchen clock joined in. Whirring laboriously into life, it progressed into seven slow, measured chimes before coughing and wheezing into silence. Only the slow *tick-tock* showing that it was still alive.

"Time to go." Pa rose, creaking, to his feet. "I'll see thee to thy stop, lass," he said, looking across at Penny. "And I'll see thee aboard before I leave."

Filled with good food and happy satisfaction, everyone was now hugging and kissing their goodbyes. Penny, turning to Nell, said, "I'll see you in the morning then. Lady Charlotte will be expecting you, and I'll ask Billy to pick you up at the stop."

"Aye, thanks Penny. I'll catch the ten o' clock if that would be good?"

"Aye, good enough. Lady Charlotte won't be pushing you too hard the first day. She'll understand, too, that you will want to reacquaint yourself with both Sally and George. Don't worry. I'll help you with the lie of the land."

Then, moving over to her friend, she threw her arms around her in a great bear hug. "Oh, Nellie," she whispered in her ear. "Aren't we the lucky ones after all? It's going to be great fun."

Returning the hug, Nellie agreed. "Yes, Penny, it will. Goodbye now, see you tomorrow ..."

Pa, scarf around his neck and warm cap on his head, now chivvied Penny out of the door and they were on their way.

Sure enough, Billy was waiting at the Pembridge stop-pony, cart, whip and all. As he helped her into the front seat alongside of himself, a large woolly head, complete with lolloping tongue and wagging tail, inserted himself between them. Penny laughed. "You're keeping him then?"

"Oh, ah, Miss. 'E's a right good lad is 'e. I wouldn't part with 'e now, not fer all the tea in China! 'E's my own Scruffy, ain't yer lad?"

At which, the most appropriately named Scruffy gave a joyous bark of assent. Now, with Penny still laughing, the pony turned and the little party began its trot up the driveway to Pembridge House.

"Eee, lass." Mrs. B was laughing as she beat a mixture of flour, butter and sugar into a bowl. "That lad! He's a good worker, I'll give him that. So no one is going to think ill of him for carting that dog around. Goes with him everywhere these days, and he takes care of him as though they were related." She laughed again, shaking her head. "Well, the poor animal's come on so well since 'e were a poor, lost skinny thing."

Sally, bringing over the tea for them all, smiled. "Well, Mrs. B, it's no wonder the animal is putting on weight–y'slide him enough spare vittles to feed two dogs."

Penny, obviously anxious to get back to her charge was blowing on her tea to cool it. "How's baby 'Lizbeth doing? Did she cry again last night?"

"Aye, lovie. Well, she misses you when y're gone–and then, of course, she's teething now so fast. Another one come through last night. Mrs. Kipps were telling me this morning." Then, laughing again, she said, "I think we'll be losing our Mrs. K soon if this keeps up. Unfair to wet nurses is this teething business, I'll tell thee that for nowt."

Putting down her cup, she rubbed a hand absently over her breasts, in remembrance of the long-ago nursing of her own twin sons, both of whom had died at eight years old of the scarlet fever.

Knowing the story, Sally and Penny exchanged glances. Sally put out a hand and grasped the older woman's gnarled fingers in her own. *She's like a daughter to her,* Penny thought. *Nellie will be so pleased to see how Sally has blossomed.*

Drinking down the last dregs of the warming liquid–short though that ride had been up the driveway, it *was* a cold November night–she put down her cup and said, "I must go up and see my little darling. Me being back will give some relief too to poor Kipps."

"Aye, lass. Y'do that then. We'll manage the cups, and"–patting the bowl–"I'll save this in the ice box 'til it's time to put in the oven for tomorrow's tea."

CHAPTER TWENTY-FOUR
A Reunion

Lady Charlotte had done her homework.

"Your sister has been telling me of how keen you have always been to obtain some scholarship."

"Yes, m'lady. But the war intervened, I'm afraid."

"Hmm ... the war has intervened with everyone's life, m'dear. It's all very sad."

Charlotte sighed. Straightening her back, she settled herself on her chair, the while regarding Nellie with interest.

Both women were seated in the small office cum sitting room that was Charlotte's private place.

Outside, a November gale was blustering against the closed window panes. Inside, a fire was dancing in the grate, sending out its flickering fingers of warmth into the room.

All was quiet, warm and cozy, and Nellie found herself wanting to sink down onto the comfortable looking chaise longue in the corner, close her eyes and drift gently away into sleep ...

Recognising this, Charlotte smiled in sympathy. "Yes." She spoke softly. Then, more forcefully, she added, "This war has sapped the backbone from us–it has been a wicked thing. But now"–raising her voice–"it is important that we gather the forces within us, and resume some kind of productive daily life."

She smiled, and Nellie, doing her best to smile brightly back, made a gallant attempt to obediently gather her forces.

Gently now, Charlotte continued. "For now, you must rest–at least for today. Penny will show you to your room, where you can unpack your things. There is plenty of space for you and the room is comfortable. Tomorrow will be soon enough to discuss your terms of employment here. I gather," she continued, "that you have already made reunion with both Penny and your sister?"

Nellie nodded, suddenly finding herself horrifyingly close to stifling a yawn.

Now Charlotte, full of sympathy, reached out her hand to clasp the younger woman's fingers.

"Oh, my dear–I *do* understand. You young people have given sterling service to this country. It is one of the reasons why Sir Richard and I have decided that you deserve a chance at some employment that would suit your present skills. This, more than would working at the mill."

Nellie nodded again, still stifling that yawn. Now Charlotte, infected by this, yawned widely herself. Both women then laughed, in a companionable sort of way.

It seemed clear that they would like one another.

Charlotte rang the small silver bell that sat between them on the table. Magically, it would seem, Penny appeared. She had, of course, been waiting.

Curtseying, Penny nodded to Nell who, taking her cue, rose and dropped a brief curtsey herself.

Now Penny, taking her exhausted friend by the arm, escorted her swiftly along the corridor and up a flight of stairs. At the top of these, she opened a door to what now would be Nellie's room.

A gasp of delighted surprise from Nell made her smile.

The room was comfortable indeed. A fire dancing in the grate, a large, comfortable-looking bed, a window overlooking the grounds– and flowers everywhere.

"That's Billy's doing," Penny explained. "He's a good lad, our Billy, even if he *is* always carting around that messy dog. Mrs. B swears that we have to clean the kitchen floor every day *twice* as many times as we had to before. But, he's a treasure–works very hard, considering the lack of help he has.

"Also," she continued, "he grew those flowers himself in the old greenhouse. He has a green thumb, right enough does our Billy.

"Now, take off your shoes and lie down on that bed. You can unpack later. Billy brought up your stuff. I'll draw the curtains so you can sleep, and I'll bring up some hot water later on, so you can wash yourself.

"Lady Charlotte said you can join in for supper tonight with Mrs. B, Sally, Aggie and me in the kitchen. It's cozy down there, and we can catch up with all of the news."

During the course of this long exposition, Penny had been steering Nell in the direction of the bed, then helping to relieve her of her shoes. Now, she gently pulled the top cover over her sleepy friend, patting it down around her.

She moved over to the window and closed the curtains in order to dim the light. Exiting the doorway, she paused to say "Sleep well," but Nellie was already sound asleep.

Smiling, Penny quietly closed the door and went downstairs.

*　　*　　*

George was sitting on the top steps of the wooden hut he shared with two others. A large part of the Pembridge grounds, now that most of the patients had left, was being reclaimed.

Come the spring, these lands would be restored to something like their former glory: rose gardens in the summer, daffodils, crocus, snowdrops and tulips in the spring. Charming arbors and hedgerows would be replaced. Borders, abundant with flowery growth, restored.

Billy could hardly wait.

The kitchen gardens, of course, had remained untouched. They had been, for the duration, supplying nutrients for the family and their unfortunate "guests."

It was around the edges of this particular piece of land that several huts had been built in order to accommodate the special group of men who, like George, were suffering from the trauma of war.

The day was warmer than it had been of late, the gift that sometimes comes to relieve us of our winter woes.

A watery November sun peered through the clouds and George, seizing the moment, raised his face to receive this benediction.

It was a different George than the one who, four years before, had marched off so gallantly to war.

He was much thinner, and the face was gaunt. He sat hunched over, as though protecting himself from the blows that the world might offer–and, indeed, that it already had.

He had been whittling at a piece of wood, and had been greatly occupied by this for the last half hour or so. Then, as the sun hid its face once more, he returned to his whittling with a fierce concentration.

Suddenly, there came a *snap* ... The wood had broken in two.

Cursing loudly, almost crying in his frustration, George tossed both wood and knife aside.

Standing, he gazed around the grounds before him. Not a soul in sight, except for Billy busily digging in a far corner of the kitchen garden. His usual companion–dratted dog–was happily snuffling around in the damp grass.

Feeling his usual, overwhelming restlessness, something that came upon him all too frequently, George decided to go for an exploratory walk.

He had been expecting a visit from Nellie. Sally had told him that she would be coming this morning.

Eager though he was to reunite with his much loved sister, the restlessness had claimed him completely, one of the many symptoms left to him by the war.

Deciding to avoid any contact with either Billy or his dog, George disappeared behind the hedgerow, making his way down the slope to a nearby farmer's field.

Leaning against the gate, he gazed across the somewhat sodden stretch of winter grass. Pulling his cap more firmly down upon his head, he adjusted the brightly scarlet muffler round his neck. He thought of Penny, knitting it for him, as he and she talked together on summer nights.

The thought of her made him smile for a moment, and he felt almost relaxed.

Scanning the field, he pondered on how *different* everything looked here. He remembered the sodden, muddy fields of France, and recalled how he had thought it so sad that these fields had once been lush pastures, just like the one before him now.

Fingering his muffler, he found himself thinking again of Penny. *How sweet she is*, he thought. He found himself wishing that he could woo her, wed her–make her his girl ...

No sooner had he begun this wishful thinking, however, than his mood darkened again into the familiar despair. How could he even *think* such a thing? Wooing and marrying was for *normal* men–not for angry, empty husks such as himself.

Reaching the gate, he swung himself over and began to walk around the edge of the field. Movement–walking, sometimes even running–seemed to be a salve to these empty feelings of his. And indeed for many of the men here, suffering from the same condition.

Lifting his head high, he began to move faster, and now faster again. *That's better*, he thought. The blood was now coursing through his veins, and he was breathing deeply of the fresh, clean air, gulping it down into his lungs.

It was only when he reached the point in the field that was farthest from the gate, that he began to realise he was not alone.

The bull, sole occupant, and Lord and Master of the field had seen *him* too ...

Moving closer, the bulky animal peered at him, the "intruder," through bloodshot eyes. Pawing the ground, snorting in disgust, he moved his massive frame towards George–lowering his head as he did so.

It was then that George became aware of yet more lively action. This was coming from the direction of the gate, where now Penny, Sally, and Nell were standing, aghast, at the sight before them. All of them shouting and gesticulating in a fever of anxiety.

They were soon joined by Billy, equally concerned. He seemed to be encouraging his dog to enter the field.

Then, Scruffy was over the gate and charging towards the bull–a great, hairy, furious canine pitting his wits against this massive enemy.

For a frozen moment, George stood watching in fascination, as Scruffy veered, first left, then right, then left again ... zig-zagging in front of the bull's face.

The bull, turning his head from side to side, was becoming increasingly bemused, and increasingly angry.

All of those at the gate were now calling to George to come. "Oh, *come* George. *Quickly*, move *now!*"

And George began to run. He ran as he had never run before in his life–not even in France.

Reaching the gate, he climbed hastily up and was promptly hauled over the top by four pairs of eager hands, where he then stood, doubled over and gasping for air.

As he began to recover, he could see that everyone was now concerned for the dog–though Penny's arm, he noticed with satisfaction, was now firmly entwined round his waist.

Scruffy seemed to be enjoying himself. Now that the man was safe, he could play at teasing the infuriated bull to his heart's content.

Billy, however, had other ideas.

"*Scruffy!* Come here this very minute! Tarnation have ye–ye miserable mongrel." This was said in a paroxysm of fear.

Registering the panic in Billy's voice, Scruffy turned to come back, and the bull, lowering his head at an angle, aimed one of his horns directly at the dog's stomach.

Simultaneously, there came a roar of fearful anguish from Billy, and a truly blood-curdling scream from Sally. The bull, distracted for a moment, lifted his head–and in that moment, freeing himself from Penny's grasp, George was back over the gate.

Ripping the bright red muffler from around his neck, he flapped it frantically at the enraged animal, taunting him with it before dropping it to the ground at his feet.

Scruffy was, by now, over the gate and being hugged by Billy. George decided that now would be a very wise moment to join him there. Leaping over the gate with an agility that he had thought must have gone for ever, he landed back over the gate and into the waiting arms of Penny, who–white as a sheet and trembling–was gazing at him with adoring eyes.

In a moment, they were in one another's arms, oblivious to the world around them. The others cheered and clapped, and Scruffy barked in concert with the general good cheer and wagged his tail. Billy, still uttering highly unrepeatable curses, was doing so in tones of great affection.

The group now moved away from the gate which, despite its stoutness, would probably be no match against a charge from the maddened bull.

He, however, was now focussing his fury on the scarlet scarf at his feet. Bellowing and pawing at it until bending, he managed to get it entangled in his horns. Unable to shake it off, he charged, still bellowing, to the other side of the field.

There, in the morning, he would be found by a *very* puzzled farmer who, as he carefully retrieved the tangled mess from the horns, would be wondering where the dickens this muddled piece of knitting had come from ...

* * *

"*Well*, that's a *good* piece of news then, lovie!"

Mam and Alice were taking a short break in their usual spot-half- hidden again by the semi-closed door. Pa, understanding the importance of the discussion the two women were having, was again keeping a discreet eye that they didn't overstay the prescribed time.

"But Jess, *Germany* ... I'll have a German grandchild soon!"

Alice was almost wailing.

"But Alice, lovie–" Mam was in a conciliatory mode. "Lovie, he's well, and he's happy, your Gary. My goodness, he's *alive*–isn't that wonderful? Let's look at that letter again."

She reached for the letter, clutched in her friend's hand. Reluctantly, Alice relinquished it and Mam began to read aloud.

> *My dearest mam,*
>
> *I'm sorry to have taken so long in getting to you, but with all of the disruptions going on in Europe at the moment, well, you can imagine, it hasn't been easy to get the post through.*
>
> *I'm sure, though, that the War Office must have informed you some time ago that I were alive and safe ...*

"*Huh.*" Here, Alice interjected with a scornful sniff, "No, they never did–dozy lot of skivers."

If Mam was mildly shocked at this unusual sort of interjection from her friend, she made no comment and merely continued with her reading:

> *As they will have told you, I were took a prisoner–me and my three horses, a year or two ago ...*

Alice nodded in remembrance, shaking her head and sighing:

> *I were lucky. Once they found out I knew a thing or two about how to handle horseflesh, they put me to work on a farm instead of sending me off to a prison camp ...*

"Well," Alice murmured, "I suppose I should be grateful for that." Mam nodded in agreement, and then read on:

> *The farm where I ended up is in a region of lush grassland. There's lots of rich pasture, so there are*

plenty of dairy farms here. Herr Grunwald, my father-in-law ...

Here, Alice winced at the thought of this new German relative that had so suddenly been introduced into her life. Mam, noticing this, hid a smile before resuming:

He breeds horses like, on the side, and I were soon put in charge of this sideline of his. He had lost his wife not long after my Gerda was born, and his son, Hans, were killed in the war ...

Here, both women exchanged glances of sympathy. "Ah, me," Alice murmured. "I suppose, in the end, it's been the same for all of us."

They were interrupted now by Pa. "Sorry, ladies–time's up. Back to the grind!" This stern comment was softened by his warm smile. As the two women heaved themselves to their feet, he briefly touched Alice's shoulder. "So glad to hear your Gary's safe," he said. And then he was gone again on his rounds.

*　　*　　*

"Ooh, you're going to be an auntie!"

Nellie was excited and wistful at one and the same time. She reached out to little 'Lizbeth, safely ensconced on Penny's knee. The baby beamed and hiccupped, blowing a milky bubble onto Penny's blouse.

Both young women laughed fondly at the child as Penny, experienced now and ever ready, pulled out a large handkerchief and wiped the child's face.

'Lizbeth squirmed in protest, uttering little squeaks and turning her head from side to side, as she tried to avoid contact with the firmly wiping hand of her keeper.

"How much longer will Mrs. Kipps be in charge of her feeding?" Nellie asked. "Shouldn't she start weaning her soon?"

"Oh, yes, I'm already mashing up rusks with regular milk once a day, and she seems to be taking to this quite well. For such a little thing, she has quite the appetite!"

They both laughed again then stopped. 'Lizbeth, as though to belie Penny's words, had been promptly sick–all over Penny's already damp blouse.

Following this, the child gave a burp of satisfaction and Penny, rolling her eyes, pulled out yet another clean wipe.

Then, having cleaned her charge, this, to more squeaks of protest and wildly waving arms, she handed the child over to Nellie, who gladly accepted her, cuddling her soft warm body in her lap.

Having cleaned herself up as best she could, Penny said, "Hmm, I think, after I've been up and changed, I'll speak to Mrs. Kipps about us giving her just *half* a rusk for a while. Piggy-wig here has bigger eyes than stomach, I think."

Both women laughed again at the use of the familiar term used by both of their mothers in times gone by.

Then, reverting to Nell's original statement, Penny sighed. "Yes, I'll be an auntie, and my mam will be a granny. I think it's lovely, but my mam has reservations about our Gary having married a German."

"Aye, it's sad really."

Nellie was automatically rocking the now sleeping child in her arms. "We've been so used to the word 'German' standing for 'enemy.' It's difficult to change course all at once."

"Yes." Penny was nodding in agreement. "It makes me wonder if they–the Grunwalds and their neighbours–feel the same. He lost his son, you know."

"Aye, but"–Nellie was determined to look on the bright side–"he's now *gained* a son, *and* a grandchild. Perhaps," she continued, "this kind of intermarriage will help people to see things in a different light. In that case, it will put an end to any more thoughts of war."

"Oh, *Nell*." Penny was laughing now. "You're beginning to sound like our Cilla! Well, I'd best be getting back to the nursery. Come with me if you would. It'll save waking 'Lizbeth before we get there *and*"–here she sniffed at herself in distaste–"I'm going to have to get changed."

"Of course. I'll come with you to your room while you get yourself sorted." Nellie gently shifted the baby onto her shoulder. Giving a sigh of contentment, the child snuggled deeply into her arms, and Nellie felt a sudden pang of love. For some reason, a picture of Harry entered her mind, but she dismissed it sharply.

By now the two women were mounting the stairs. "Oh good. Thank you–that'll be helpful." Penny was pleased. "I've been wanting to ask you ... How are you finding George these days? How's he responding to his treatments?"

Pausing for a moment, stroking 'Lizbeth's back, Nellie thought carefully before replying. "Y'know, it's interesting, he's having the same treatments as the other men, but I don't *think* that that is the thing that's making the improvements he's been showing."

"He *is*, isn't he–making improvements." Nellie smiled at this eager interjection from Penny.

"Yes, he is. Of course, there are good days and bad days, as with all of them." Penny nodded gravely in acknowledgement. "But," Nellie continued, "it's something else, another relevant factor that I think is more important than all of the mechanical manipulations of the medics ..."

Pausing for a moment, biting her lip, she continued. "I really don't mean to criticise. The doctors are caring, and working very hard at trying to find the best treatment possible for these poor men, but ..."

She paused, and Penny, buttoning up her fresh blouse, looked up. "But?" she prompted.

Taking a deep breath, Nellie went on. "I know that to some extent ... well ..." She corrected herself. "Actually, to a quite considerable extent, they resent my 'interference.'

"After all, who am I? A simple mill girl turned VAD nurse. I don't have a degree. I'm flying by the seat of my pants as they say in the air force, but ..."

"But what?" Penny was gently lifting the child from Nell's arms as they spoke. 'Lizbeth made a murmuring sound as she cuddled into this fresh breast. Though still asleep, her lips were moving in a seeking manner. She would need the ministrations of Mrs. Kipps very soon.

Making their way to the nursery, the women paused on the landing. "So, what d'you think?" Penny asked. "What *is* it that is making a difference in George's case?" She raised her eyebrows in concert with the verbal questioning.

Smiling broadly, Nellie replied, "Well, of course"–she wagged her finger in mock reproach–"you *know* that, for a start, it's *you* ..."

Penny had the grace to blush, then quietly admitted, "I know."

"Well"–Nellie was frowning in concentrated thought–"the thing that brought about your connection, *finally*, was the shock of nearly being killed by that wretched bull. Of course, what caused his condition in the first place, was the series of shocks from watching his comrades killed or maimed during that terrible time in France. We both remember what that was like."

Penny nodded vigorously, remembering only too well what it was like.

'Lizbeth began to stir restlessly awake, searching urgently now with her lips. Penny cuddled and shushed her then said, "But what else d'you think it might be? I really would like to know." There was a wistfulness in her tone that roused Nellie's sympathy.

They continued now down the corridor that led to the nursery. Nellie, thinking hard, chose her words carefully. "I can't be certain, but the vigorous movement, the running and then jousting with the bull-all of that combined with his anxiety for Scruffy and the urgency of his feelings for you ... well ..." She sighed. "It-it just *seems* to me that it's shaken him out of the deep despair that was holding him back before."

They had reached the nursery door, and now 'Lizbeth was asserting her needs in no uncertain tones, wriggling and wailing in infant disgust that her hunger was not being attended to.

Nellie, smiling, turned to go, but then turned back for a moment. "I feel as though I'm on the verge of some kind of discovery. *But* ... I can go no further. I don't have a degree."

She turned to go.

Penny, her hand on the nursery door, called after her. "Then you must go and get a degree!"

*　　*　　*

"Now, my dear, please, make yourself comfortable."

Charlotte and Nellie were in Charlotte's cozy sitting room. A fire was glowing in the grate, and Aggie was on her way up with one of Mrs. B's delicious teas.

It was a bitterly cold day in mid-December, but despite the fire, despite the thought of tea, Nellie was not at ease.

"Please, do sit."

Obediently, Nellie sat, bracing herself for whatever might be coming.

"Now, my dear, as you probably know, I've been discussing your work with Dr. Fielding."

Nodding miserably, Nellie took in a deep breath, then slowly let it out.

"I believe that you have been somewhat at odds?" Charlotte was smiling pleasantly, but her look was searching.

Now, Nellie thought. *It's now or never.* "I can't prevaricate, Lady Charlotte," she began. "I must ... I must speak as I find."

Charlotte nodded. "Please do, my dear. That is what this little chat is about."

Little chat? Nellie mentally shook her head. *Little chat!* Then calming herself under the expectant gaze of her employer, she set out to explain herself. "Dr. Fielding is a fine man and an excellent doctor. Obviously, he knows far more about the ... the *mechanics* of this sort of thing than do I."

As Nellie paused, Charlotte nodded, making a "Please continue" kind of gesture.

"The thing is, Lady Charlotte"–Nellie was now warming to her subject–"the thing *is* that though he might think me to be just an ignorant mill girl, I am not! I have done quite a lot of reading recently, mostly the writing of Dr. Sigmund Freud of Vienna.

"His writings mesh somewhat with my own experiences at the Front and, with respect, unlike Dr. Fielding I have *been* there. I have shared the circumstances that these men have endured. I have shared their mental pain derived from watching their fellow fighters torn apart by gunfire, by landmines, by fire from above ... and then they have had to return to the Front and continue the fight as though nothing had happened. If they collapse in mental disorder they are despised as cowards, as shirkers of their patriotic duty ...

"But oh, Lady Charlotte, they are *not* ... they are *not* ..." Her voice had been rising in the passion of her discourse, and now Charlotte was leaning forward, her eyes shining. She was riveted by this young woman before her. She opened her mouth to speak, but was interrupted by a timid knock at the door.

"Come in." Charlotte's voice was husky with shared emotion. She cleared her throat.

The door opened and Aggie entered, carrying a tray laden with the goodies of afternoon tea.

She had obviously heard the passionately raised voice and been alarmed by it. She moved across to the table and, at Charlotte's instructions, deposited the tray in front of her.

Then, with a demure bob of a curtsey and a murmured, "M'lady," she departed–but not before casting a worried glance in Nellie's direction.

Nellie could only guess at the gossip that would soon be pervading the kitchen area, and could only hope that Sally would not be too worried.

Charlotte took a composing breath before lifting the pot and pouring.

"I can see"–she was choosing her words with care–"why Dr. Fielding and his colleagues have been worried by you."

Nellie's heart sank. Has all that she has tried to impart meant *nothing* then?

Seeing her face, Charlotte hastened to reassure her. "My dear, you are most certainly *not* an 'ignorant mill girl.' You are, as I have suspected from the beginning, a bright, clever young woman who deserves to have more clout than you have. Now, tell me, if you would, exactly what *your* treatment theories are."

Hardly believing this dramatic turnaround of events–she had been quite sure that she was about to receive her dismissal–Nellie opened her mouth to speak.

She was laughingly interrupted by Charlotte. "But firstly, let us enjoy this delicious offering of Mrs. B's and drink our tea before it cools. Then you can speak. Between mouthfuls of course." The injunction was primly given, but there was a twinkle in her eye.

*　　*　　*

"Well, m'dear, this is rather a large jump you've made. What gave you this idea? After all, Fielding was most positively against the idea of keeping the girl on."

Sir Richard and Charlotte were in the library, Richard's favourite place in the house once he had finished with the business of the day.

"She is, after all," Richard continued, "only a mill girl. It was most kind of you to take her on in the first place ..."

"Oh, *Richard!*" Charlotte's tone was reproachful. "No one is 'just a' anything these days. This war has helped to change people's attitudes considerably."

As her husband opened his mouth to speak, she rushed onwards with enthusiasm. "Besides, Sally is from a mill family, but just look at the talents she is showing in the kitchen these days!"

Reluctantly, Richard, savouring in retrospect the delicious braised beef and apple pie from the night before, had to agree. He nodded, adding, "Mrs. B is an excellent teacher, I must say."

"And Sally is an excellent student. Remember, too, young Penny. Look how invaluable her services have been to this family."

Richard, feeling cornered, sighed. "But, m'dear, Fielding is most adamant that the Parkin girl is an intrusive meddler–a confusing influence on the men."

"Richard, *darling,*" Charlotte took a deep breath before continuing. "I, like Nellie, have been doing some reading. Much of what I have read reflects the ideas for treatment that she is espousing. *And,*" as her husband opened his mouth again to speak, she continued firmly, "as far, for instance, as George Parkin is concerned–as well as one or two of the other men–there seems to have been some marked improvement in their mental stability."

"Oh?" Richard was a reasonable man, one who knew his wife to be no fool. "What is it you two have heard that Fielding, the expert in these matters, has not?"

Charlotte smiled. She was not about to become confrontational; there was too much at stake. "It would seem"–she was picking her words carefully–"that even among the experts, there is some division of ideas."

She paused, frowning, she *must* get this right. "Well, there seem to be two main streams of thought. The most prevalent, is the one currently held by Fielding and his colleagues." Here, she shifted in her chair, settling herself comfortably into her discourse.

Recognising the symptoms–he was about to receive a lecture– Richard sat back in his chair, fingers steepled, the very picture of an attentive listener.

"This theory," Charlotte continued, "is that these men are suffering from 'shell shock.'" Richard nodded and his wife went on. "The notion is that this is an understandable, but strictly temporary, condition. The men were treated and given a brief respite before being *returned to the Front,* where they were expected to function as normal–if anything that happened at the Front could *ever* be described as 'normal.'"

Her voice had risen in her incredulousness as if, in speaking of the situation, as opposed to the reading of it, had lifted these ideas off the paper and into real time. Richard, sensing his wife's anger, nodded again in encouragement.

Taking a deep breath, Charlotte continued. "Some men, indeed, do go on, fighting and surviving as they watch their comrades dying in droves around them. It is only later that the symptoms recur with, as we can see right here and now, devastating and seemingly permanent results."

Richard was now leaning forward, regarding his wife intently. "And the other theory?" he asked.

"Well–" Charlotte was grateful at feeling her husband's support. "Well, there are some observers, medical and otherwise, who refute the very name 'shell shock.' They find that the men who seem not to have recovered at all, even following a short period of respite, are experiencing something much deeper–a dislocation, if you will, of their emotional stability, even while their sense of reasoning is left intact.

"These are labelled as cowards, shirkers of duty–even, by some, as *traitors*!" Her voice had risen again in frustration. She was beginning now to understand Nellie's stance and finding herself to be more and more in tune with it.

"You see," she went on, "there seems to be nothing wrong with their powers of reasoning ..."

"Oh?" Richard was fascinated.

"Yes, it would appear that they are made to believe what they are told–that they 'ought' to be over the shock by now. That their minds are 'just fine' and that they must now snap out of it.

"Those of good conscience believe what they are told–that they must be cowards who are deliberately avoiding their duty. This leads them into depression. Depression leads to anger which, when turned in upon themselves, leads to more depression, self-doubt and finally, anguish ..."

"And this young woman understands all of this?" Richard was having trouble meshing his notion of the "mill girl" with his wife's understanding of Nellie as being "a bright spark," as he would put it.

"*Yes*, Richard." Charlotte was absolutely positive that Nellie was a *very* "bright spark" indeed. "She was able to prove to me that these ideas work, especially where her brother was concerned. He now knows that he is loved, and he no longer feels himself to be the hopeless outcast that he once thought himself to be.

"Penny loves him, his family loves him–even Billy's Scruffy loves him!"

She smiled, remembering Billy's "Oh, m'lady, y'should just see them two together. Never seen the like of it!"

"Hmm, and what, pray, does Fielding think of all of this?" Richard was puzzling the pieces together in his mind. He had, after all, invested a considerable amount of money into this medical experiment.

Charlotte sighed. "Well, as you will have gathered from his reaction during my interview with him, he is not at *all* pleased. Nellie has tried to be as circumspect as possible, has tried to not outwardly oppose his methods, *but* their methods *are* absolutely opposed.

"She believes in fresh air, in vigorous movement, in convincing the men that they are *not* cowards, and that they are certainly not mad. As I've already said, she assures them that their reasoning is intact. It's their *emotional* well-being, their nervous systems, that have been compromised and that therefore, it is this that must be given the attention from their healers."

She paused for a moment, before saying softly, almost to herself, "It's a wonder that these poor men are not all stark raving mad, after the things they've seen and experienced at the Front ..."

Seeing her distress, Richard moved to her. Sitting beside her, he wrapped an arm around her shoulder.

Smiling a little shakily, she reached across her body, lightly resting a hand upon his.

"The problem is that Fielding and his cohorts are utterly convinced that strapping their patients into chairs and applying electrical shocks will adjust their reasoning. Instead, this kind of treatment *confuses* their reasoning, and attacks their nervous systems. The results, then, are absolutely opposite to what is wanted. Nellie believes strongly that in most cases at least, electrical stimulation is *not* the way to go about things."

Richard could not help but smile at his wife's passionate espousal of the "mill girl's" ideas. He refrained, however, from sounding disrespectful. "So, this is the young woman whom you would like us to support through a university degree." This was a statement, rather than a question.

Charlotte turned to him, her eyes shining. "*Yes*, oh yes, Richard darling. I truly believe that she has it in her to succeed."

"But–" her husband had a proviso. "Firstly, she will have to have at least a year's worth of tutoring–Latin, mathematics, physiology *and*"–as Charlotte made to interrupt–"in the end, she will only have learned the same ideas that Fielding has. So, of what use will that be?"

"Oh, Richard, she will be able to mesh what she learns with her own ideas. Indeed, they are not only *her* ideas. There is a movement afoot in the world of psychology that has helped us to understand these things. By the time she reaches the university, she might just find that these notions are slowly being accepted more readily into academic thought."

Richard opened his mouth again to speak, but Charlotte forestalled him. "As far as the tutoring is concerned, we could use Professor Faulkner again. He certainly managed to get Robert into university, reluctant though he was to go."

Richard sighed. For just a moment, a vision of rapidly disappearing pounds, shillings and pence flashed before his eyes. But then he thought, *Well, Fielding will be pleased to get the girl off his back.*

Feeling cheered by this thought, he said, "Very well, m'dear. We'll consider this to be an experiment in social progress. The tutoring will commence after Christmas and, if the young woman manages to make the grade, we will provide her with a scholarship that will get her through the course."

Charlotte clapped her hands in joy.

Richard continued, a smile upon his face. "Speaking of Christmas–what d'you think of us inviting our delinquent son back into the fold?"

Suddenly, Charlotte was a young girl in love again. "Oh *Richard*, you are the *best* husband in all the world!"

Throwing herself into his arms, she kissed him with a passion that was instantly returned.

Pounds, shillings and pence? Richard thought to himself. *Pah. This is worth it, every penny ...*

*　　*　　*

It was Christmas Eve, 1918. Bill and Jessie Parkin–Pa and Mam–were sitting at the kitchen table at 85 Nanton Street. The kettle was on the hob, getting ready for the making of tea.

Mam sighed. "Eee, Bill, lovie. Christmas won't be the same wi'out family around–not even Alice and Isobel; what wi' Alice in Germany, and Izzie having to work late at Pembridges, and then staying wi' friends for Christmas Day."

She sighed again, looking so doleful, that Pa felt that he must cheer her up. "Well now, m'lovie. Ain't it just wonderful that Alice is over there with the Grunwalds? That he invited her was very generous, and bodes well for her and Gary, for his Gerda and the babby that is so near birthing."

Mam sighed again. "Aye, I suppose so. Very nice for them all."

This was said wistfully and with a slight edge to it. Pa, touched, thought he detected just the slightest note of the little green god of jealousy. Tenderly, he patted her hand, lying listlessly on the table top. "Aw, lass. We'll be grandparents soon enough–just you wait and see."

"That's just it. We've waited and waited, and now, with all this talk of university and it taking six years before she's finished, our Nellie won't be ready for *ever* so long."

She was near to tears and Pa decided that he must be firm. "Jess, my lass. You know as well as I do that our Nell has a gift for learning."

Mam opened her mouth to speak but Pa, determined to make his point, overrode her. "What we have to think of now, is what *Nellie* wants. Not so much of what *we* want, but our Nell."

"What a wonderful gift." he continued, "Sir Richard and Lady Charlotte have offered her. Why, 'tis a chance in a million!"

"Aye." Mam sniffed. "And where did the money come from in the first place for them to be able to give her this *gift?* It comes from our work at'mill. Years and years and *years* of it. So don't talk to me about any 'gifts,' Bill Parkin. T'aint no gift to me."

Pa was shocked, and rather disturbed at this outburst. He had never heard this kind of talk from his wife before, and was now quite distressed.

"Oh, *Jess* ..." He sighed, shaking his head in an "I give up" sort of way.

Now, it was Mam's turn to feel sorry. Reaching across to her husband, she said, near to tears, "Oh, my Bill. I'm sorry, lovie. I've just been so worried about what will become of us all.

"There's our George, still not really quite himself. Our Sal–doing very well to be sure, but stuck for the most part in t'kitchen in that place. What time does she have to be social at all? Then, there's our Will ..."

Interrupting, Pa reached again across the table. "There's always the chance that he will come. He said in his letter he'd try."

"Humph!" Mam was not so sure. "I think, Bill, that our boy has turned into a bit of a will-o'-the-wisp. He seems to be comin' and going hither and yon ... having too good a time in London to bother wi' his old parents."

Pa tightened his grip on her hands with both of his. "Now, now, my Jess. He's young. He's been through a terrible time and deserves to be let be to kick up his heels a bit among the bright lights."

The kettle had begun to whistle and bounce upon the hob. Automatically, Mam began to rise.

"Nay, m'lass. I'll get it." Pa was on his feet and crossing to the stove.

While he busied himself with fetching the cups and pouring hot water from the kettle to the pot, he said, "Well, they'll all be comin' for a visit once the Christmas rush is done, I s'pose. Y'can just imagine what it must be like up there for t'staff–what with all o'those men still there, and the doctors and the Countess Marchmont. Sad about her husband dying and all." He handed his wife her piping hot tea, then sat down to enjoy his own.

"Hmm." Mam sipped, and then said, "From what I've heard, the woman is well rid of him."

Pa raised an eyebrow at the lack of charity in his wife's tone. He wisely refrained from comment, however, understanding that this mood of hers was coming from a deep sense of disappointment.

The clock on the kitchen wall began to wheeze into life. It was about to announce that it was now 4 p.m.–the first hour of Christmas, according to the Christian calendar.

Christmas had now arrived.

Smiling, Pa whispered, "Happy Christmas, my lovie." He was about to take another sip of tea when there was a loud *rat-a-tat* on the door.

Mam exclaimed, "Now, who can that be?" Pa shuffled across to pull the bolt. The door opened and a resounding "*Happy Christmas, Mam and Pa!*" was heard.

Will was standing on the doorstep, a happy beam upon his face. His arms were full of presents.

Behind him stood a shadowy figure that Pa didn't recognise. He was obviously with Will, however, so wordlessly, too full of emotion to speak, Pa beckoned both of them in before closing the door behind them.

"*Will*–oh, my Will!" Mam was up, and all aches, pains and bad mood vanished, was flying across the room to greet her son.

The presents were knocked to the floor in the vigour of Mam's embrace. This, Will returned with equal enthusiasm.

The other man bent, along with Pa, to pick them up. Handing his load over to Pa, he smiled shyly–at the same time sharing a look with him that clearly said, *Ah, mothers* …

Pa decided that he liked the look of this stranger, now opening his mouth to speak, but Will, still holding on to his mam, turned apologetically.

"Mam, Pa," he said. "This is someone I met in London. He has nowhere to go for Christmas so, as he's a friend of our Nell, I took the liberty of inviting him."

Then, more formally, he declared, "Mam, Pa, this is Harry–Harry Briggs."

CHAPTER TWENTY-FIVE

Harry's Story

It hadn't been easy at first. Bill and Jessie Parkin had taken him in, of course–it would be unthinkable to turn away a stranger from the door on Christmas Eve. At the same time, they were almost overwhelmed with joy at the return of their very own Will.

The rejoicing was great indeed that night, and very soon, was being shared with several of the family's neighbours. Jessie, though, had found herself to be missing Alice–now experiencing her first Christmas in Germany.

Harry, seated on a bench beside the fire had watched longingly. It had been a long time since he had been sharing such joy with family. Even on the next day–Christmas Day itself–and despite the sharing of small gifts, good food and good, cheerful company, he could not dispel a strange kind of emptiness in his soul.

How, he was wondering, could Nellie ever forgive him? He shivered inwardly at the thought of the possibility of her walking through that front door and despising him ...

The Parkin parents had been very kind, refraining at first from mentioning his apparent desertion of their daughter. Will, though, had clapped him on the back declaring–several times as the wine flowed–that "Our Nell has a right stout heart. If she loves ye, she'll have ye." Then, with a twinkle, he'd added, "Aye, lad. She'll have you, whether you will or not!"

Everyone had laughed at that. Even Harry had to smile at the sheer exuberance of this delightful family.

Later, in the evening of Christmas Day, however, Pa had broached the subject. Mam and Will were finishing up the dishes–Mam busily plying Will with question after question regarding her son's war experiences.

Will, fondly amused, was doing his best to tell an interesting story, the while carefully omitting the more gruesome details.

Pa, carrying two glasses of fine Scotch–another generous present from Pembridge House–handed a glass to Harry, before pulling up a chair and planting himself down beside the young man.

"Sláinte." He raised the glass and Harry, smiling at the appropriately Scottish toast, raised his.

"Sláinte," he returned, and they clinked glasses before taking a first mouthful.

"Aah." Pa leaned back, smacking his lips in appreciation. They sipped again, Pa looking over his glass at Harry.

Realising what might be coming next, Harry lowered his glass. Taking a deep, steadying breath he began. "Sir, I expect that you must be wondering why I'm here now after ... well, after ..." Faltering before Pa's steady gaze, he took another gulp of his Scotch.

"After you left our Nellie at the Front." Pa's voice was not accusatory, more encouraging the young man to continue.

Blushing, Harry looked into his glass, seeking the right words to explain. Then, looking up, he said quietly, "You all deserve an explanation–especially Nellie–but honestly, I can't find the words to explain. I wish I could."

Seeing his quite genuine distress, Pa reached for the bottle and topped up both of their glasses. "It's alright, lad. I'm not going to bite yer head off. Nell showed me your note. Sounds to me like someone who was at his wits' end. And God knows, from what I've heard of this war, and what I've seen of so many of those who've come back maimed in mind as well as body–and this includes our George ..."

"Aye!" the heartfelt interruption had come from Mam.

Looking up, the two men saw her now sitting at the table, one hand firmly clasped over one of Will's, sitting quietly beside her, the other holding a glass of sherry, also a gift from Pembridge House.

"Aye, lad." Mam raised her glass. "Our Nellie understands how badly you must have felt. She were hurt at first, y'know ..." Here, Harry winced, taking another gulp from his glass. "But she came to understand that y'had to get away and think."

"*Yes!*" Harry placed his glass carefully beside him on the floor. "Yes, that's *exactly* it."

And then, the story came tumbling out as Pa, Mam and Will listened quietly.

He told them of the fact that he was a pacifist–always had been, always would be. This was said firmly and with conviction; nevertheless, he had felt that somehow, he must play some kind of a part to help out those men fighting for their country. And so, he had volunteered as a stretcher-bearer.

The other three nodded. They knew all of this from Nellie. They all owed him, though, the chance to continue at his own pace.

There was a moment's pause as he collected his thoughts. Pa offered the bottle, indicating with a raised eyebrow, *More?* Harry shook his head, while Mam smiled in approval.

"I'd been working on the Western Front for several months," Harry now continued. "Then I met Nellie" His face softened in recollection, and the two parents exchanged approving glances.

"This has been a terrible war" It was almost a whisper. Suddenly, his body clenched in a spasm, two black holes of darkness before he burst forth with "I couldn't help it, you see ... I just couldn't see any future. Not for us, not for me, not for *anyone* in that Godforsaken place."

Mam moved automatically to comfort, but Pa put out a restraining arm, his look saying without words, *Let him get it all out.*

Nodding, Mam sank back in her chair. Out of the corner of her eye she saw Will–all previous bonhomie vanished. His body was clenched in rapt empathy as he shared Harry's pain.

His mother shook her head. Looking across at her husband, she saw that he, too, had noticed Will's reaction, and was equally moved by it. *Dear God*, Mam thought, *let there never be another war like this.*

There was a brief silence as everyone waited for Harry to continue. Instead, his body loosening, he bent forward in his chair. Placing his hands over his face, he began to weep in great, gasping sobs. His face turning from side to side, he scrunched it into his hands as though trying to tear away his memories.

Now, there was no stopping Mam, and Pa had the sense not to try.

Rising from her chair, she threw herself at the agonised young man before her. Seeing that she was about to kneel, Pa grabbed a cushion and threw it down in front of her.

Kneeling now beside Harry, she reached her arms around him, rocking and crooning as she would to a distressed child.

The weeping slowly subsided into a series of hiccups as he tried to apologise.

"Nay, lad. Nay." Pa was now on his feet and raising Harry up from his chair, patting his back as he did so. "Thou hast *nothing* to apologise for. Our Nellie knows that now. She understands what thou"–and here, his glance included Will–"have all been going through. Never fear."

In the end, they were all sitting around the table, as the rest of the story came tumbling out.

Having left the immediate vicinity, he had moved several stations down the line, offering his services to other field hospitals. Offers that were gladly received.

Very soon, however, it became obvious that the hunt was on. Cilla's emissaries were in hot pursuit of his whereabouts. Part of him was almost glad of this. Nellie loved him enough to seek him out and he was tempted to turn around and go back ...

But then, there was a raid, and another raid and another.

Dead and wounded men, Germans and Allies alike, were piling up now in numbers too awful to contemplate. Numbed and deadened in spirit, the bearers and medics had laboured stolidly on, sans food, sans rest, sans hope, until they too began to drop, and were dispatched homewards on sick leave.

With the hounds on his tail, Harry decided that now was the time to break away entirely. In the dead of one night, his backpack on his back, he left the camp and set off into the darkness, not knowing, not caring where he was going.

Travelling mostly by night–it was easier to stay hidden that way–he had slowly moved on in a south-easterly direction.

There were, of course, no road signs. They had all been either destroyed or moved to other areas, pointing in the wrong direction, this in order to confuse the enemy. Harry had to rely on the positions of the sun–a difficult enough task when one was travelling mainly by night.

To make things even more difficult, not only were the signs missing, but there was scarcely any road left either. There was just a mess of churned-up mud, hardening now in the coming winter's cold.

Once, during a full moon, he found himself in the middle of what must, at one time, have been a charming small wood with a stream running through it.

Instead of trees, however, all that was left were charred and broken stumps. He could easily visualise the smoke rising from them as some battle raged around them--the enemy searching for any sign of desperate men seeking shelter from this storm of fire, then destroying them completely, in the mindless, careless way of battle.

Sighing, Harry, thirsty from his nights journeying, moved towards the stream in order to fill his canteen. As he approached, his nose, attuned now from his days and weeks of living "wild," twitched. There was an odour--no, a *stench* that, as he recognised what it was, made his stomach churn.

Looking into the stream, he could see by the moon's light a tangle of bodies. Some were burnt beyond recognition. All, apparently, having been driven into the water, seeking it as an alternative to being burnt alive.

Instead of turning away, Harry drew nearer to this scene of horror. Something inside him demanded that he record every single detail.

Now, he knew that somehow, he would live to tell this tale. It would be his job. Whatever higher power, whatever God there was willing, he would survive. He would write, he would speak. He would *make* people understand the depth of inhumanity of man to man that is spawned by war ...

The moon, heedless of all below, slipped then behind a cloud and Harry turning, grim-faced, but with a back as upright as a ramrod, marched forward on a journey that was now filled with purposeful intent, and he began to work his way back, in the direction from which he had come.

He still hid by day in ditches, behind barns--most of these now ruined and abandoned, but some, occasionally still in use. In these, he was able to spend a somewhat more comfortable night.

Grateful beyond measure for the comparative warmth offered by other living creatures--cows, goats and more rarely a donkey, even sometimes, an ancient horse--he would wrap his jacket around him, cover himself with straw and, resting his head on his pack, would fall deeply into sleep.

There was a movement from Mam, and Pa, looking at her, could see the grim intensity of expression on her face. He knew, from long experience, that that look indicated her intense desire not to cry, but to wait for the moment when she would be needed to succour and to comfort.

Quietly patting her hand, he moved to rise, noticing as he did so, Will's face.

Pale, and rigid with concentration, his son's eyes were fixed upon Harry's face in total absorption. Every now and then, his head would nod slightly in agreement, while his lips moved wordlessly.

Dear God, Pa thought, *whatever have these boys seen? Will they ever feel at peace with themselves, ever again?*

Shaking his head, he moved to the sideboard and picked up the half-empty whisky bottle. Without asking, he filled Will's glass, then poured some into Harry's.

With a raised eyebrow, he silently motioned to his wife, nodding at the sherry bottle. She shook her head no.

Will had absently picked up his glass and, still not removing his gaze from his friend's face, was quietly sipping.

Harry seemed not to have noticed the refilled glass before him.

Well, Pa thought, *it'll be there when he needs it.*

Sitting down again beside his wife, he picked up his glass and drained it in one gulp. *God,* he needed that!

Resuming the thread of his story, Harry told of how now, he was feeling more at ease, risking moving--albeit carefully--in the daytime. He was hungry, yet also feeling unwell.

For days now, he had eaten only what he could root out of the ground. Unharvested potatoes and, more occasionally, carrots were abundant. The farmers themselves either dead or having fled the area.

These "fruits of the earth" had, of course, been not at their best by now, having been thrown and tossed from the ground by the unheeding activities of war.

It was these scatterings, peeled, but entirely raw, that had sustained him for the duration of his journey until that time.

Mid-day, and rain beginning, he'd suddenly felt *really* ill--his stomach rebelling at last, against the inadequate diet it had been forced to accept.

Here, Mam nodded, with an expression on her face that said *No wonder* ...

Gathering his strength, Harry had moved on.

The rain, now pelting through the rapidly defrosting mud, he had suddenly felt violently sick, vomiting right there, where he was standing. At the same moment--*Oh, dear Lord, no*--he felt the sudden gush of his bowels rapidly emptying.

Now, he knew he could go no farther. Feeling truly ill and repulsed by his now unsanitary condition, he squelched on, peering anxiously through the obscuring curtain of rain, seeking out any sight of shelter there might be.

At the sight of a barn, he thought, he would crawl in amongst the straw and quietly die.

Now Mam, her face expressing the tenderest compassion, reached out a hand towards her young guest. Harry gratefully returned the grasp.

CHAPTER TWENTY-SIX
Joy to the World

"The lad's still sleeping, I hope?" Mam was bustling with breakfast preparations.

How does she do it? Will asked himself. Yawning, he nodded then, "Aye, and snoring like a drainpipe an' all!"

Pa, stoking up the fire, laughed. Turning to his son he cast a quick nod towards his wife. "Nay, lad. There's no stopping her when there's family matters at stake--always been the same."

"Humph." This, a snort of derision from Mam. She was, however, smiling. More seriously now, though. "We'll let the poor lamb sleep for a while longer. He were right exhausted after finishing his tale last night, and no wonder."

Turning to her son, she asked, "How much of all this did y'know about before, lad?"

Will, already pouring tea, shrugged. "Well, quite a bit, but not really all those details that coom out last night."

He began spreading butter on the toast that Mam had handed him and, at the same time, stirring both porridge and tea with the same spoon.

Mam noticed this with raised eyebrows, but she refrained from making any comment. Later would do.

Will continued. "As I said on Christmas Eve, when we first coom in the door, we met up in London--at the pub actually. We got chatting, and discovered that we'd been covering the same ground, more or less. So, finding ourselves with a lot in common, we had much to talk about and decided to take up with one another, as friends like."

"Hmm. Well I'm glad y'did, lad. Our Nellie will be most pleased, I'm sure, to meet her Harry once again." This, from Pa, while Mam smiled and nodded in agreement.

Mam sat for a moment, sipping tea, then said, "Talking of our Nell, as soon as we've finished breakfast, we'd best be getting on w'dinner preparations. I've got the bird, all ready to go, and the pudding--God bless our Mrs. B--is wrapped and ready for the steaming pot. Will, you can get on with peeling the vegetables, and I'll start getting the table dressed and ready for company."

She beamed, proud of her plans for dressing the table, then sighed. "Aye, it won't be the same w'out Alice here. I miss her. Eee, but she's happy where she is, I'm sure. Mebbe they'll all be over from Germany next year. Now wouldn't that be nice!

"Still, we'll have Sally, Penny, and Izzie, then George, if all is well." A shadow crossed her face, but then she cheered. "Aye, well, our Penny will sit wi' him, God love her. She and our Nellie between them have done wonders with his confidence.

"Oh, yes. And, of course, there's Harry and our Nell ... Ooh"-she was hugging herself now, visions of a happy marriage and of grandchildren making her eyes sparkle-"I do hope that all goes well wi' the pair of them!"

Pa started to speak, but Mam, now in "commander" mode, continued with her orders.

"Pa, you can go and fetch some holly from the back patch--oh, and when y'say the grace, don't forget to give thanks for them monks what found Harry and saved his life in the monastery hospital."

As Pa again opened his mouth to reply, Mam, now on a roll, and clutching his arm, continued, "Oh, and we mustn't forget the farmer what found him in the first place-eee, wheeling him in a barrow, covered in sacks!"

She shook her head in half humorous, half scandalised, and wholly pitying sympathy.

Pa, knowing better than to interrupt his wife when she was in this organising mode, merely drew himself up to full height. Snapping into a brisk salute, he murmured a low "Aye, aye, mon capitaine," while he and Will exchanged a wry smile before setting obediently about their various assignments.

There followed two hours of extreme busyness in the Nanton Street kitchen, but finally all was ready.

The scent of a delicious Christmas dinner being cooked wafted through the entire house. The pudding, wrapped in cloth, was dancing in the copper that stood in the scullery behind the kitchen, and fronds of holly adorned the mantle.

As the ancient clock began to wheeze its way up to the striking of the hour, Jessie Parkin descended the stairs.

Smart new skirt and blouse, this one of the presents from Will, adorned her matronly frame, and she had also exchanged the food-stained apron of the morning for a fresh, clean one.

The family, including now Harry, burst into spontaneous applause. Blushing, Mam waved them away with an "Eee, get on wi' yer, the lot of ye." But everyone could see she was pleased.

Smiling broadly, Pa swiftly produced a twig of mistletoe from behind his back and waved it at his wife with an interrogative tilt of the head.

This was met with yet another "Eee, Bill, away wi' ye then." But she was blushing with pleasure just the same.

With a mock expression of disappointment, Pa turned away to tack the mistletoe just above the front door entrance. "That'll do for the young'uns then," he said, winking broadly at Harry, who now was blushing furiously himself.

As the clock gathered itself together with a *Bong*, announcing the hour, Will moved over to the front door and, opening it, looked down the street. Then, swiftly withdrawing his head, he announced loudly, "They're coming, eee by golly by gum, they're here!"

Then, puzzled, he looked out once more, waving to the small group approaching the house. "Eee, but there's a young lad with 'em. A young lad and a great galumphing hairy animal of some sort."

Exchanging looks, Jessie and Bill rolled their eyes to the heavens.

"Eee, I forgot to mention it," Mam said. "Our Nellie asked me a while back if young Billy might be allowed to come, and where young Billy goes, so goes Scruffy. Well," she added, "the wee beastie *did* save our George's life. So, he's welcome."

The front door was now opened wide to greet the arrivals, and at the sound of their voices, Harry had turned deathly pale.

Sensing the young man's panic, Pa moved towards him. Grasping Harry's shoulders with a comforting arm, he murmured, "Nay, lad. All will be well. Rest assured. All will be well."

And then, the room was filled with chattering life. Scruffy, entranced by the wonderful smells of food, was prancing round the room in an ecstasy of pleasurable anticipation.

His tail was wagging furiously, knocking at the furniture. As the restraining hands reached out towards him, he licked at them with unrestrained and enthusiastic love.

Mam and Pa were kissing and hugging Sally, Penny, Izzie and George, then warmly shaking hands with an embarrassed Billy, as he apologised profusely for the rampant Scruffy.

The only stillness in the room was coming from Nell, still standing in the doorway and Harry, frozen, at the foot of the stairs.

As the commotion of greetings began to subside, everyone else, now sensing the stillness, quieted down, turning to look. Even the dog had calmed, moving towards Billy he sat, gazing up at his adored master with an enquiring look. Then, at a motion from Billy's hand, he collapsed at his feet with a patient sigh.

Now, all was quiet. It would seem that the very room was holding its breath.

Slowly, Nell, her arms beginning to stretch out to her Harry, moved towards him.

Their eyes locked. Harry took two swift strides and they were in one another's arms. Wordlessly holding fast one to the other.

Both Mam and Pa's eyes were filled with tears, and Penny, turning to George, snuggled into his arms.

Both couples were now kissing, very gently, before standing back to look at one another in wondering love.

Izzie, moved, glanced at Will standing alone and somewhat forlornly beside the door. Smiling, she moved towards him. Holding out her hand in greeting, she said, "You must be Will. I'm very pleased to meet you." Gratefully, Will returned the grasp and held on to the offered hand.

Sally moved towards Billy, and smilingly, he put an arm around her shoulders, giving them a gentle squeeze.

"*Well!*" Pa swiped at his cheeks. "Well, my Jess, it seems that that mistletoe isn't needed for these young 'uns. How about you and me making good use of it then?"

Laughing, Mam slipped an arm through his as they marched purposefully towards the mistletoe hanging above the door. There, they kissed, a gentle, tender long-married kiss, while everyone else cheered.

At the sound of cheering and laughter, Scruffy, released from the imposed stillness at Billy's feet rose, shaking himself back onto his feet with a *woof* that declared *And about time, too. Just give me a piece of that goose.*

The laughter continued as they all seated themselves around the table.

THE END

CPSIA information can be obtained
at www.ICGtesting.com
Printed in the USA
LVHW091531190921
698208LV00007B/1252